# Life's
## *hidden*
# Treasures

*A Joyful Heart*
*is Good Medicine*

An
Irish Woman's
Heritage

# Life's
## *hidden*
# Treasures

## Rose Marie Rivard

Tate Publishing & *Enterprises*

Published by Tate Publishing & Enterprises, LLC
127 E. Trade Center Terrace | Mustang, Oklahoma 73064 USA
1.888.361.9473 | www.tatepublishing.com

Tate Publishing is committed to excellence in the publishing industry. The company reflects the philosophy established by the founders, based on Psalm 68:11,
*"The Lord gave the word and great was the company of those who published it."*

Book design copyright © 2009 by Tate Publishing, LLC. All rights reserved.
*Cover design by Lance Waldrop*
*Interior design by Stephanie Woloszyn*
Cover, personal, and family photos property of Rose M. Rivard.

Published in the United States of America

ISBN: 978-1-60696-385-2
1. Biography & Autobiography / Cultural Heritage
09.02.23

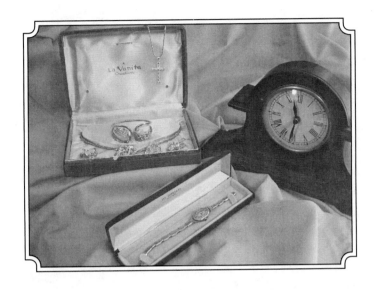

Special Remembrances
As told by

Rose Marie Rivard

# Dedication

This book is dedicated to my children, JoAnn, Joseph, (Mary) Jane, as well as all our grandchildren and great grandchildren to come.

A special thanks to my wonderful husband, Joe. Without his love and generous support, many of these precious memories could not have been made.

Come and journey with me through the life of a courageous woman named Katherine, as seen through my eyes and written from my heart.

# Introduction

Why did I feel that this day was so special? Why did it seem that this particular visit with Mom was more meaningful than ever? Why did the stories that she told of her life seem more caring and wonderful to me?

The sun was shining brightly in our home on this late September afternoon. My husband, Joe, had just returned home with my mother. He picked Mom up from my brother's house as he had done many times before. Mom was up for the summer months living with my brother, Roland, and his wife, Bertha. In these later years, Mom spent winters in Florida in a home that she and Dad shared before he died. My brother brought her back home to Michigan late in the spring. This gave her family the opportunity to spend time with her and renew our love and friendship.

I was looking forward to having her over for dinner today and was preparing a special meal. Mom seemed very happy as she entered our home. I greeted her with a hug and a kiss and told her how wonderful she looked! Mom was attractive and looked young for her ninety-one years of age. She had beautiful white hair, kept short and curled. She was small by nature but had a very big heart. Mom always had a smile for all and never spoke ill of anyone. I rarely remember her being in a bad mood, and age had not changed her disposition. In fact, it had brought her added grace and dignity.

As I was in the process of preparing dinner, I asked her if she wanted to peel potatoes. Mom said yes, as I knew she would. She loved to help out in the kitchen when cooking. Peeling potatoes was her favorite job. When it came to doing dishes, Mom always wanted to wash and I was to dry. Being together in the kitchen again reminded me of the many times we spent together as I was growing up. We were a large family of three boys and three girls. Mom always cooked big meals. That meant we had plenty of work to do helping her. Mother's dinners always consisted of a meat, potatoes, vegetable, and homemade bread or biscuits. These were hearty and staple meal characteristics of her heritage.

Mom seemed very peaceful today. She was enjoying our kitchen work as we prepared dinner together. I asked her to cut some pineapple into small pieces and mix it with cottage cheese. She proceeded to cut them up into little bits. She tasted it and told me how good it was. We both sensed joy and contentment working side by side. I had planned some of her favorite things to eat. We were having chicken, which I had cut into bite-size pieces for her eating convenience. By preparing the meal in this manner, it would save us both awkward embarrassments. Mom prided herself on her independence. Even at the age of ninety-one, she felt she could take care of herself. Not to honor this strong desire would hurt her greatly. We also had potatoes, green beans, and tomatoes (for my husband). Mom didn't eat tomatoes. "Too much acid," she would say. She believed that tomatoes would cause her skin to break out in a rash. Mom was concerned about taking care of herself, despite her age.

When we finished dinner, my husband left the table to read his paper. This allowed Mom and me to be alone. We would have another of our quiet talks as was our custom. We always began our talks at the dining room table and finished them in another part of the house. Typically, we would take our tea with us. Drinking tea had remained one of Mom's simple pleasures. It endured throughout her lifetime. She always credited her love for drinking tea to her Irish heritage. She said in the "old country" everyone drank tea. Coffee was not the customary drink. Consistent with our Irish ancestry, we enjoyed having our tea together.

Today we chose the living room to finish our talk. The sun seemed so welcoming and inviting in the front of the house. The living room was very bright and cheerfully decorated with soft whites, pinks, mauves, and greens. In one corner of the room stood a tall grandfather clock, which Mother loved to hear chime. The sun came streaming through the lace curtains of the bay window and bounced off the mirrored wall, casting rays of light everywhere. This wonderful light created a mood of peacefulness and welcome warmth, despite the coming of fall and a chill in the air. Mom and I both knew that she was to leave for Florida in a couple of weeks, and our time together was drawing to a close this year.

Mom had chosen to sit in the green rocker today. She didn't like to sit on low chairs because it was difficult for her to get up from such a position. Mom was enjoying the mood unique to this particular day. It was rich in contentment, restfulness, and happiness. She was eager to tell me once again the many stories of her early childhood in her homeland and her voyage to America.

I looked into the mirrored wall across from me and I could see both our reflections. I wondered how I was going to remember all of her stories and the many special times we shared together. I realized what a wonderful gift her talks were to me. I sat down on the sofa opposite her so that we could be near each other. Snuggling into the sofa, I began to listen once again as she walked me through the years.

# Chapter I

Katherine Ellen Starr was born on March 8, 1900, in Woodford, Ireland. Woodford is located in the county of Galway. She lived with her parents on a farm near the River Shannon. She had a great love for the many green hills which could be seen for miles around. Over time they became very special for her. In her later years she referred to them as the "beautiful green hills of Ireland." As a child, Katherine loved to take walks with her father over these hills to visit her grandfather. She also enjoyed her many walks near the River Shannon. These events helped create fond memories of her early childhood in Ireland.

Katherine's parents were John Starr (born in 1869) and Anne Hayes (born in 1874). Her father was born in Derrygoolin and her mother from Clouhoola. John and Anne were married in 1899. Anne descended from several generations of farmers in Ireland. She was from a family of six children. Katherine's father was from a family of four children with less of an agricultural background. John's father was Michael Starr. Michael worked in a local mill until he was injured. He descended from three generations of Irish stock. Before that, Katherine remembered her father telling her that his family originated from Spain. They were a very musical family who loved to play concertinas and violins.

After Katherine's parents were married, they lived on a small farm in a thatched-roof house made of field stone. Her uncle Pat had built this house for her parents. Their home sat down in a valley where you could look out and see the beautiful hills. In addition to the thatched roofing and field stone walls, it featured a cement floor. Inside there was a living room, two bedrooms, an upstairs loft, and a large kitchen. The kitchen had a huge open fireplace. The bathroom was outdoors (truly an "outhouse"). Drinking and cooking water were brought inside the kitchen by bucket, filled from the outdoor well. Evening light was provided by kerosene lamps. The lamps were used very little as they went to bed at sunset and were up at sunrise.

In addition to the house, the modest farm included two small barns. One barn served the cows they had, as well as a few pigs and one horse. The other barn sheltered the small flocks of chickens, turkeys, and geese. Scattered about inside the barns were assorted farm implements. They were well used but of great value to a poor farmer. There was never money for new farm equipment.

Implements were handed down from generation to generation. Katherine was born on this farm with the assistance of a local mid-wife. Likewise, each of her eleven brothers and sisters would come into this world in similar fashion.

Her family was poor, but Katherine felt that she never lacked the necessities of life. Their clothing was very plain. The peasant dresses hand sewn by her mother came from material bought in the town of Woodford. Katherine and her sisters would wear field bonnets with their dresses. Even the bonnets seemed plain. Printed dresses and bonnets were only worn for Sunday best. Her brothers would wear hand-sewn shirts and store-bought knickers for Sunday best. These mid-length pants were worn with long, dark socks. Coats or jackets were not customary. Long skirts, shoulder shawls, and heavy woolen sweaters were typical. Children in Ireland always received clothing as Christmas presents. Toys were uncommon, and the few they received were homemade from items used around the farm. There was little time for play, but the children didn't know any different way of life.

Katherine was the oldest of twelve children. This left little doubt that she was expected to take a big role in helping out around the house and in the fields. There were always chores that needed to be done. Her father did most of the outside work, but Katherine was expected to work inside the home as well as helping her father outside. Because her mother was bearing newborns almost yearly, she was unable to help Katherine with much of the work. Katherine's life was hard and her work endless, but she was never one to complain. People in Ireland were either rich or poor. A middle class did not exist. As most of the people she knew were poor, Katherine felt that everyone lived the same way.

Early in the morning Katherine would arise and start baking bread for the day. The fireplace was used for cooking and baking. Her mother taught her how these things were done when she was tall enough to reach the kitchen table standing on a stool. She was about five years old at the time. The bread would be baked in the very large open fireplace. The fireplace had racks which allowed you to put your pots and pans on to cook and bake. Katherine cooked meals for the family, as well as baking their bread.

The fireplace was the center of their small home. With all of the food being constantly prepared throughout the day, the kitchen was always a busy place. The large open fireplace was not a luxury but a necessity. In addition to its usefulness in the preparation of the daily meals, it served as the family's only source of heat.

Ireland is a very rainy, damp country, and the sun refuses to shine a great deal of the time. While it rarely gets extremely cold, it does require heat year around to take off the ever-present chill. Turf (a sod-like fuel) was used to burn in the fireplaces. Because her parents' farm consisted of about fifty acres of rolling green hills, turf was readily available. Katherine and her oldest brother Michael would go onto the hillside with their father to cut the turf from the ground. Taking the horse and wagon, they would load up several weeks' supply of the precious fuel. They would then return, unload the wagon, stack the turf, and allow it to dry. The turf would be wet or very damp when it was first cut and would burn more efficiently when dried. This was best accomplished by cutting the turf into eight inch squares. These were stacked in pyramid-style so that when the rain came it would easily roll off the turf and remain dry.

Katherine enjoyed being outside with her father. She was very fond of him. Their time together seemed to pass by too quickly! Her father had a favorite nickname for her. He called her Katie. She still remembers the laughter they made riding or walking about the green, rolling hills. The joy and the warmth that they shared together lightened the burdensome routine of household work. Despite the demanding lifestyle and her many responsibilities, Katherine never complained. "Hard work never hurt anybody, that's just the way life is." That was one of many favorite expressions Katherine used throughout her life.

The farm was the family's complete source of food supply. The Irish climate was conducive to farming. There was a large garden to raise vegetables, and they were able to harvest more than one crop per year. Multiple crops ensured that food was plentiful. With this particular kind of growing season, "canning" food was never a necessity.

Parsnips, cabbage, and potatoes were a few of the fresh vegetables that they raised. They would store extra hardy root vegetables in a dirt cellar to keep until needed. Leafy vegetables were kept where it was coolest, near the dirt cellar floor.

Some of Katherine's chores included milking the cows and churning cream to make butter. Chickens, geese, and turkeys were used for eggs and meat. Extra eggs, meat, butter, etc., were taken to the village to sell in order to buy flour, kerosene, or clothing material.

Whenever a family needed meat, all the men would gather at a farm to help with the butchering of the pigs or cattle. The meat would be brought into the kitchen to hang by the fireplace. It was smoked near the fire to prevent spoiling. It was necessary to smoke the meats as there was no refrigeration on the farms at that time. The beef was frequently divided up between two or three neighbors who were in need. Hams and bacon were kept for the families themselves. As the meat was being smoked, it sent an aroma throughout the rest of the house. This evoked a continuing memory for Katherine, and she said she could still smell the meat being smoked in her father's house.

In addition to the community sharing in the preparation of the smoked pork and beef, there were many other examples of the way in which unity within the small rural farms was demonstrated. For example, each farmer had only one horse to help cultivate the vegetable garden. Poor farmers couldn't afford two. Whenever there was plowing to be done, another farmer would share his horse, as two horses were needed to plow the fields. All the families worked together. For Katherine, growing up in a community where people helped each other in a sharing, cooperative manner was a natural way of life.

The closest village in the area was named Coose. It had only one grocery store and a mill. This was where Katherine would walk, carrying eggs and butter to sell for the items they needed at the time. There was little need for money. The farm sustained them. It was about a four-mile walk, but Katherine's father would intercede with horse and wagon in the event of rain. Woodford was the largest town within walking distance of their home (several more miles beyond Coose). In Woodford people would buy larger supplies for their families. When buying supplies for the month you would bring the horse and wagon and transport the precious cargo home.

Katherine and her father (along with her brothers and sisters) walked every Sunday to Woodford where the church was. Her family was Catholic. Most all of the families in Southern Ireland were Catholic. On Sunday mornings they would get up very early and put on their best Sunday clothes. It was a long walk to church and back. It would take all morning and into the afternoon. Katherine did not realize at the time that she was developing a great faith and trust in God. This would see her through a lifetime of trials and hardships. Her entire family had been baptized in Woodford. Most all of Katherine's relatives were buried in the cemetery there as well. The Catholic parish in Woodford is still an active parish today.

Katherine would enjoy Sundays with her brothers and sisters away from much of the daily farm work. Katherine especially enjoyed spending time with her father. He was always kind and gentle. He would make them laugh, and he loved to sing! They spent a great deal of time singing together as they walked to and from church. She remembered well his favorite song "Danny Boy." He had a grand voice and Katherine was blessed to have inherited his singing talent. Throughout her life Katherine's favorite song to sing would also be "Danny Boy."

Irish folklore and folk songs speak to the hard times that the people suffered through. Irish music is rich in love of country and love of God. It took great endurance just to survive the many hardships these people were confronted with. Not all Irish folklore was sad, however. There were many stories of finding Leprechauns. They were portrayed as little old dwarfed men dressed in green. If you saw one you could gain a hidden treasure. They were very hard to catch! If you saw a rainbow after a rain shower you really needed to go looking for one. *Ah, surely ye know now, 'tis a pot of gold at the end of the rainbow and only a wee Leprechaun can take you there!*

These legends were told to children to lighten the burdens of the day. These were the kind of stories

Katherine's father told her as they walked to and from church. He had taught his family the most important lesson in life. Recognize your blessings. He believed they were blessed because they had a roof over their heads, clothes on their backs, and food on the table. The Irish are very proud of their heritage, and Katherine typified such pride. Music and song helped perpetuate this cultural pride and seemed to soothe the Irish soul.

The family dinner took place after Sunday Mass. This meal was a special highlight. It usually consisted of chicken or turkey with all the trimmings. Before leaving for Mass, it was usually Katherine's responsibility to select the fowl. She would break its neck with her bare hands and place it in hot water so the feathers could be plucked with greater ease. Her mother would then attend to the final preparation and baking while the older children traveled with their father to and from church services.

In addition to walking to church there were daily walks to Derrygoolin School. Katherine would walk to school with some of her brothers and sisters. They would meet many of the neighboring children along the way. She enjoyed the company, but it was a long walk! There was no one near Katherine's age to play with, but she looked forward to being with the other children anyway. It seemed as though the children were always working, and it was difficult to find time to play or socialize with other children your age. Katherine never had a need for dolls because she was always taking care of her younger brothers and sisters.

Katherine was in the third grade when she and her brother Mike had to quit school. There were too many things that had to be done on the farm. As the oldest children in the family, Katherine and Mike were needed to meet these family obligations. Despite Katherine's interrupted schooling, she was able to learn to read and write well enough to continue her studies on her own. Often she would help the smaller ones with their school work, and this would reinforce the things she had learned in school. While Katherine felt the loss of a continued education, she understood that few children in circumstances similar to hers ever had a complete education. It was far more important to be able to work.

The only medical doctor in the area was found in Woodford. Because of the distance, he did not make house calls into the country. For most types of sickness you became your own physician and had to get well by yourself. Only in severe circumstances would someone be taken by wagon to Woodford. Katherine's first brush with serious illness came early. Mary Ellen (her little sister) became ill with the "croup." There was little the family could do, and she died at the tender age of five.

Katherine would soon encounter death again when her little brother Tom died as she held him. She was only nine years of age. Her mother had gone into town with the horse and wagon to get supplies. Katherine stayed home to care for the younger children. Tom had been sick, but her mother felt that Katherine could care for the child as well as she could. Katherine was cradling Tom in the rocking chair to bring him comfort from his crying when he went limp in her arms. She knew he was dead. Katherine laid the baby in his cradle and ran outside to the barn to tell her father. Early experiences such as these gave Katherine wisdom regarding the value of life. It also taught her perseverance which would allow her to survive life's many difficulties. While life went on, Katherine would never forget how it felt to have someone you loved and cared for die in your arms.

Some of Katherine's happier times included visits to her grandfather's house on the weekends. After he had been injured at the mill, he had a stroke. He was unable to care for himself after that. It became a weekly custom for her father to shave him and help with various chores around his home. She and her father would walk over the hills and through the woods to get there. It was often night upon returning, and it was Katherine's special joy and privilege to be allowed to carry the lantern. It was quite a walk, but Katherine enjoyed these times alone with her father.

In addition to the many times of walking, talking, laughing, and singing together, Katherine remembered vividly her father's fiddle playing. Many times on a Saturday night at her grandfather's house the neighbors would gather for an evening of food, singing, and square dancing. These were often held with no special occasion in mind. Her father would play the fiddle along with a couple of their neighbors. They would play their way into the night while the neighbors would get Katherine up and dancing! This is how Katherine learned to dance. She truly enjoyed listening to her father sing while playing the fiddle. These were very happy times for Katherine. The dances at her grandfather's house became special times for her. Birthday parties and the like were nonexistent, and these dances filled a valued place in her heart. Katherine's grandfather died at the age of sixty-eight when she was eleven years old. She deeply missed the walks she made with her father to his house. There was so much joy and merriment in the festive atmosphere of his home.

While Katherine has fond memories of her father, she remembers her mother less favorably. Many times her father would take the older children out into the night to go to their grandfather's house. These were times when Katherine's mother would treat the children so badly, her father was afraid she might seriously hurt them. Sometimes they would have to stay away two or three days until their father felt her mother's temper had calmed down enough to bring them home. Unfortunately it seemed that because Katherine was the eldest, she was the most frequent child to have to leave. Katherine speaks of her mother as having "bad spells" and remembers it was not safe to be around her during those times.

Around twelve years of age Katherine left home to

learn a trade and work in the town of Woodford. Her father provided her with a small amount of money to attend Derryover Cooking School. The fee was one shilling per day. Shillings are similar to American pennies. One shilling was equal to two pennies. She recalls the first meal she learned to prepare was rabbit. From skinning and cleaning, to cooking and presentation, she was diligent in her tasks. She attended Derryover with fifteen other students, all of whom were girls. When it was Katherine's turn to cook for the day, she had to pay for all the items she needed to prepare the food.

During her apprenticeship she earned room and board with a nearby family. The people that Katherine first worked for were school teachers. They had a son who was crippled and needed care. Katherine was responsible for the cleaning and cooking, as well as helping the mother take care of the crippled boy. For services rendered, Katherine would be paid the sum of one pound per month (about 55 cents), and given the upstairs loft to sleep in. If Katherine had any money left over after meeting her personal needs, she would give the money to her father to help out at home.

Katherine's early life in Ireland was hard, and poverty seemed everywhere. Jobs were few and advancement seemed impossible. Katherine's teen years were void of dating experiences, and she never had a boyfriend. There was a proper time for dating and marriage. These experiences would be "arranged" by her father. It was common at the time that Irish girls didn't marry until their mid-twenties. Men married in their early thirties.

Katherine spent the next eight years going from one job to the next. She worked for different families who needed help cooking, baking, or helping to care for small children. She would always keep in contact with her family and would visit them from time to time. However, she never went home again to stay. From the early age of twelve, Katherine was on her own. One must wonder if she really ever had a childhood.

There seemed little future for the young and aspiring. Dreams of success were daunted by continual work, eventual marriage, inevitable children, more work, and finally death. Her family was poor even in the best of times. By the 1900s when Katherine was born, Ireland had not fully recovered from a potato blight that started in 1845. Potatoes were the staple food for the Irish farmer. When the crops were blighted, there was terrible suffering. It was estimated that one million people died of starvation. Many of the farmers in Ireland were wiped out, and their family was no exception.

Katherine remembered her grandfather (on her mother's side). He had lost his farm and had no place to live. He carried his few belongings in a sack along with some straw made from wheat. He traveled from place to place visiting family and friends. He would spend a few nights at each one's house. When he stayed at her parents' home, Katherine remembered him opening his sack at night. He prepared his bed of straw on the floor in front of the fireplace. Even though Katherine was very young at the time, she realized the hardships people in Ireland were enduring.

Katherine recalled stories about men who would steal food to keep their families from starving. If the men got caught stealing so much as a loaf of bread they would be put on prison ships bound for Australia. These families would never see their husbands/fathers again. Stories such as these carved deep impressions of hopelessness upon the young people in Ireland. What would the future hold for them here? What would be their quality of life?

Because of the hardships in Ireland, there was an estimated one million people that flocked to America in the late 1800s. Ireland had more people migrate to America than any other country. During her teen years Katherine would hear talk of different people leaving for America. This was a country where men and woman alike could get jobs and advance in society. The common belief in Ireland was, "You didn't have to remain poor in America."

Katherine had two aunts on her father's side that left Ireland and traveled to America. Before they left, they discussed with Katherine's father and mother the possibility of her journeying to the United States to meet them at a later date. Her uncle Pat (on her mother's side) promised he would save some money so that Katherine could one day make the voyage. Katherine could have an opportunity to live in such a great land! Katherine remembered there were many such conversations as she grew older.

Katherine's goal was always to better herself. Her constant desire was to get ahead in life and not be a burden to anyone. She believed that hard work and a willingness to take chances was the only way to achieve this goal. She was a woman with very progressive ideas!

Finally the day came when her uncle Pat forwarded the money to Katherine's father for her fare to America. Her father sent word to her, and Katherine gathered her few belongings and went home to see her family and to say goodbye. If Katherine's life was successful in America, she would send money home for one of her sisters or brothers to come. They too would have an opportunity to come to America!

Her father took Katherine to the train station in Woodford. He made ready the horse and wagon so Katherine would be rested for the long journey that lay ahead. They rode together making small talk, neither of them wanting to speak about what was really on their minds. Would Katherine ever see Ireland again? Would she ever again see her family? Would she ever see her father again? Katherine dearly loved him and she would miss him terribly. She felt the emptiness within her grow, and promised she would always remember the good times they had shared together. Katherine admired her father. He was a good role model for her, and she believed she gained her inner strength from him. She would miss their talks together and the walks they had going to her grandfather's house. She would greatly miss the square dances and her father's fiddle playing along with his wonderful singing. These were precious memories. Katherine promised herself she would never forget her loving father.

The two of them rode together as far as the train station. It was very difficult for Katherine to say goodbye to him. After tears and hugs they parted. Perhaps it was best that Katherine didn't know she would never see her beloved father again.

The train took Katherine to the ocean port of Queenstown. She paid for her ticket and waited to board a small fishing vessel. The small boat would take her out to a large English ship called the *Coronia*. It waited in deep waters. Katherine was filled with many emotions. She was leaving the only life she knew and would be separated from her family and her country. She was embarking upon what seemed to be a very uncertain future. Katherine clung to the railing of the fishing vessel and looked back. As it departed she realized she had never seen such rough waters. The ocean before her was vast.

Some distance from the shores of her homeland she became very concerned. Katherine began drawing on her great faith in God. He would take care of her, guide her, and see her through. As she boarded the *Coronia* she wondered what the future would hold. She stayed on the deck of the ship until she could no longer see her homeland. As it faded in the distance she choked back tears of sadness. Would she ever again see the beautiful green hills of Ireland?

The date was July 11, 1920. Katherine was twenty years old and beginning a new life. Katherine didn't know anyone aboard the ship and had many concerns. She started to think the unthinkable. What would she do if she became ill onboard? Who would take care of her?

The *Coronia* was now bound for America.

# Chapter II

The large English ship headed out into the deep ocean waters. Katherine's apprehension was apparent. What awaited her next? Katherine had never traveled before and had few expectations. There were some very unpleasant realities to be discovered. The ships that traveled from Europe to America at that time were unsanitary. They were overcrowded, dirty, and provided very poor food. Ships of that day were not the luxury liners tourists would be accustomed to today.

Katherine soon discovered that almost all the people on board were men. This was a freight ship and carried very few passengers. Beyond her father, brothers, and local family neighborhood men, Katherine had not mixed with many others. She noticed the men seemed to argue and fight with each other a great deal. She was concerned about this. Traveling alone, it made her quite uncomfortable. Katherine was also aware that few people spoke English on board. She wondered how she was going to communicate with others if she needed any help. She felt a need to be protected from the many wandering eyes that seemed to stare at this very young and attractive Irish Colleen traveling alone.

As she was pondering this dilemma, she became aware of another problem. Having been on board only a short time she was starting to get seasick. Katherine began to feel rather forlorn but also believed God would help her through this ordeal.

A few hours passed and Katherine met the only Irish/English-speaking family aboard the ship. They came to her rescue. The father and mother had a daughter a little younger than Katherine, and they took her under their wing. Katherine was beginning to see her faith in God confirmed. It was this same faith which gave her courage. Katherine believed this family was aboard the ship to look out after her. Over the years she would refer to this family as a "Godsend." This became one of Katherine's favorite expressions whenever she felt the need to explain the goodness of God in times of need. Katherine was very grateful for the loving care and concern that she received from this family.

Katherine was seasick the entire trip. She could keep little food in her stomach except for a few small sugar wafers. To this day, whenever Katherine sees a wafer cookie, she cannot bring herself to eat one. The memory of her seasickness is brought immediately to mind, and she loses her appetite.

Katherine felt the days were endless. She had never seen the ocean before. It was so vast, encompassing, and unfamiliar. Experiencing the distance in this journey made Katherine realize how she wished to be once again near the banks of the River Shannon. With its huge waves, the great ocean rocked the large ship as if it were a cradle. There were a couple of nice days when she would go for a brief walk on deck with her adopted family. Most days the weather did not cooperate. There were many storms throughout the voyage accompanied by very forceful winds. Waves would wash across the deck rocking it to and fro. Because the winds were very strong, Katherine didn't feel strong enough to walk about. Those who did venture out onto the deck had to hold onto the ship's railings so they wouldn't be swept overboard. Katherine had little to do and was essentially confined to her cabin. With each new dawn that appeared on the horizon, Katherine recognized she was one day closer to America.

The voyage took eight days and nights. Her ocean-crossing experience was not a pleasant one. She missed her family and her homeland. She especially missed her father. Katherine knew her father wanted her to find a better life. He was also concerned for all those that would come after her. She wanted him to be proud of her accomplishments. Katherine was very thankful that Uncle Pat had sent the ninety dollars for her fare to America. She realized that other people had made many sacrifices for this trip. She understood multitudes wanted the opportunity to come to America but would never have the chance. So many others had life even more difficult. Katherine was being given the chance to better herself. Her strong desire to live in America helped her endure all the hardships she was experiencing. She vowed never again to feel sorry for herself. She knew that coming to America would be worth all of her sickness and loneliness.

After over a week at sea, the *Coronia* drew near the American coast. Excitement broke out among the passengers. As the ship entered the American harbor in New York, everyone gathered their few simple belongings. They wanted to be on the top deck to view the Statue of Liberty as they passed by. When the Lady Liberty came into view many cheered and waved. It was an overwhelming scene. The Statue of Liberty symbolized hope for a better life. America was the land of opportunity. So very accurate and true were these words addressed to the weary travelers. "Give me your poor, your tired…"

Excitement was at an all-time high. Everyone was happy to see this new land that would become their home. Katherine was now part of a new breed of people called immigrants. For the immigrants, America meant a better way of life with new beginnings. Many of them brought with them their different trades and talents. Others brought with them their strong desire to learn new skills so that they could advance in life. America held hopes and ideals for the immigrants that would be impossible to fulfill in their homeland. They had left behind unemployment and starvation. They had made it to America and were determined to do their best for the families they left behind.

On July 19, 1920, the ship docked at Ellis Island. People began saying their goodbyes to the new friends they had made aboard ship. Katherine felt a great deal of gratitude toward the family who had looked out for her. They promised each other to keep in touch.

Leaving the ship, Katherine wondered once again what her new life would bring. She drew comfort from the fact that she was to be met by her two aunts. Before leaving Ireland it had been arranged by her father that she was to live with them until she got herself settled in this new country. As Katherine stepped foot on American soil, feelings of pride and joy filled her. Katherine was ecstatic. She found it hard to explain her feelings to anyone. She often said it was indescribable. Katherine knew she would love America. This was the land of opportunity.

Ellis Island is a tiny island located in New York Harbor. It is a symbol of freedom for anyone who comes to America. Upon disembarkation, the immigrants had to go through a process of paperwork and physical exams. If your paperwork was in order and you passed your physical exam, you would get a landing card. The landing card allowed you to leave the island. This was necessary before anyone would be released to waiting families or friends.

It only took a few minutes for the physical, but because there were so many people from many different ships, it seemed to take forever. The lines appeared endless as each person waited their turn. The next step was an interview station where legal officials asked questions. This is where you presented your paperwork and were asked where you intended to live and work. Again, the lines were very long. It was July and very hot. The immigrants anxiously awaited their turns. Many seemed sick. Never in her young life had Katherine seen so many people! She thought everyone in the world must be coming to America. As each person completed the process they were put in a holding area. You waited there until family or friend would come for you.

While a gateway to freedom for many, Ellis Island also elicited fear. Not everyone was allowed to stay. Traveling on the ships caused many to become seriously ill and many died. Some immigrants had to be quarantined because of their sickness, and families were often separated.

These circumstances caused a great deal of heartache, disappointment, separation, and rejection. Some of the travelers were deported. For many others, however, the voyage to America concluded with great finality. Most immigrants were pleased that disappointment and sadness were not met by all. Many families were united with relatives who had made the journey before them. As Katherine witnessed the process following her arrival to America, she was extremely thankful that she had a place to live with her aunts. She believed she would find work and wouldn't have to return to Ireland. Katherine's excitement to be in America was tempered by her displeasure toward the treatment given to the immigrants. She felt they were herded like cattle in a pen and not always shown kindness.

Katherine had to wait in the holding area until her aunts came for her. She waited a long time, as they were late. While waiting she had time to wonder about her new life. How long before she would find a job? Would she make enough money to live on? Each immigrant was expected to come to America with twenty-five dollars. This money was supposed to keep them going until they could find work and start supporting themselves. Would she be able to save enough money to bring over another member of her family? Would she make friends her own age? Would she find a husband and make a life of their own? Katherine had no idea how marriages were arranged. In Ireland her father would have been the matchmaker. Who would do that for her here?

It was getting very late and Katherine was getting concerned. She wondered what was going to happen to her if they didn't come. Where would she go? She didn't know anyone she could turn to. Katherine pushed aside these worries and refused to dwell on them. She was determined that they would come for her. She believed God was watching over her, keeping her in His care.

Finally her aunts did arrive! They explained the train

was late in getting to New York from Boston. Katherine was very happy to see them. After some very joyful greetings, they left in a hurry to get to the train station. Katherine and her aunts traveled by streetcar. Katherine had never seen a streetcar before and enjoyed the ride. Along the way Katherine saw many wonderful sights. Large, tall buildings called "skyscrapers" left a deep impression on her. These did not exist in Ireland. Then there were the automobiles (more commonly referred to at the time as "horseless buggies"). Katherine had heard about cars and seen pictures of them, but this was her first time to see them for real. What excitement! She was thrilled to see the many wonderful new things in America. Katherine saw houses that were "stuck together" as she remembered. They were also quite large. She found the housing amusing compared to the small thatched roof homes in Ireland. Was everyone rich in this country? So many people had such wonderful material possessions. Life was certainly going to be different here. The immigrants aspired to become "Americanized," and that included Katherine.

Katherine soon learned that immigrant families and friends of the same nationality lived in the same areas. This helped newcomers continue with their language and customs. It also helped them adjust to the new country. Little Italy, Little Ireland, etc., sprung up across the country. Katherine learned that many of the Irish people went to settle in the Boston, Massachusetts, area. That is where her aunts lived. Many immigrants who came to America brought with them a wealth of talent and trades that would help shape the future of the country. This is why America has been referred to as the "melting pot" of the world.

Katherine was in awe as she traveled to her new home in Boston. As she arrived at her aunts' home, she was overjoyed. They lived in one of the large homes with three levels. Katherine's room was on the third floor. At the time she thought that very unique. As Katherine climbed the stairs several times a day, she soon found it to be very tiring. In the evenings Katherine loved to look out the window and watch the men turn on the street lights with a key. Katherine felt the lit streetlights made the nighttime seem so pretty. People would stroll up and down the sidewalks for their evening walks. Imagine walking down lighted streets! Such a concept was novel. This was unheard of in the "old" country. Gazing out her bedroom window in the evening provided Katherine with a few quiet moments. She reflected on all she was experiencing. She was very happy and wondered what lay ahead.

It didn't take long for Katherine to get her first job. She was hired to put eye-glass lenses into frames. This required her to use a punch press operated by foot. This was a new experience. Her aunts feared she might lose her foot because she didn't have any experience working machine presses. Katherine was very careful and managed to do the job successfully. While at her new job, Katherine met a girlfriend. She and her friend would walk to work every day. Finally, a friend her own age to talk to!

Katherine paid room and board to her aunts. She also saved some of her money. Her savings were put aside so that she could bring over one of her brothers or sisters to America. She lived on the little that was left. Katherine loved America and was happy with her early accomplishments. After a few months, Katherine felt she was doing well.

Unfortunately, soon after being hired, she and her friend were laid off. They had to look for other work as there were no unemployment benefits of any kind at that time. Between Katherine's aunts and the neighbors next door, they searched the want ads in the papers. Katherine found another job very quickly. She got a job as a cook. She felt very comfortable with this as she had experience cooking in Ireland. Katherine was employed by two schoolteachers. She no longer would live with her aunts now, as she stayed nights where she worked.

Another job experience would be in a different part of town. Katherine went to work for a doctor and his wife. They had a son who was studying to be a priest. They lived in a large house with servants. Katherine served as the main cook for the household. She was very fond of this family and they were very fond of her. The mother of the house looked upon Katherine as a daughter. Katherine stayed there for quite a long time. Working this job allowed her to save enough money to bring her sister Anna over from Ireland. At last she had a family member with her in America!

Anna went to work for the same family as a chambermaid. Both of the girls wore maid uniforms that were supplied for them. Katherine thought it was wonderful to live with her sister. The two girls became quite fashion conscious in their new life. With what little money they could scrape up they would buy store-bought clothing. This was the age of the "roaring twenties." The Gibson girl look was in and the latest hairstyle was called the "bob." Katherine liked this new hairdo and got her hair cut in this fashion.

The 1920s were an exciting time for this young country. It was a time of growth and new development. The First World War was over, and change was in the air. The immigrants that came to America with their many talents would force changes in the American way of life. It is estimated that twenty-four million immigrants came to America from other countries between the years 1800–1900. When Katherine left for America, she didn't realize at the time how fortunate she really was. In 1921, America put a ban on the massive flow of immigrants to this great country. Many of the immigrants became unemployed and were starving here too. They lived in very poor housing called "tenement houses." There were many other societal problems that surfaced. Child labor, the woman's right to vote, prohibition, a proliferation of unskilled labor, and the movement toward labor unions were a few of the many issues confronting the American people. All of these issues were controversial and challenging. Demand for social change was initiated by the government. President Woodrow Wilson was in office at the time Katherine came to America.

America was becoming very industrialized. Automobiles were now everywhere. Electric appliances were being used in the kitchens. Radio broadcasts were heard, and motion pictures were coming on the silver screen. Telephones were in many homes. These luxuries were available for the average American and not just for the very rich. In the "old countries" there were two types of people, rich and poor. America was becoming uniquely middle class.

Katherine had been in America four years. She was twenty-four years old in 1924. Would she ever meet a "special man" to marry? Katherine was a petite and pretty young woman. She was five feet and three inches tall, weighing about 118 pounds. She had medium brown hair with blue eyes.

Anna and Katherine had an occasional day off together. On one rare Sunday they went to the beach for the afternoon. It was a beautiful day and they walked a long distance to get there. They were accustomed to walking as girls in Ireland, and they didn't want to spend the money it would cost to take the streetcar. Upon arriving at the beach, they went into an ice cream store. Anna was in a mischievous mood and pretended to milk an "Elise the Cow" poster that was displayed as an advertisement for Borden's ice cream. Both girls laughed and were enjoying the humor of the moment. Meanwhile, two men had been watching them. The girls had caught their eye. The sight of two lovely young ladies being silly made these young men want to go over and talk with them. As the men approached Anna and Katherine, one of the men said to the other, "I want the one with the blue hat." Katherine was wearing the blue hat, and this is how Katherine first met Bill. He walked her home that day, and they had a grand time together. They continued to see each other whenever they could.

Katherine had never dated anyone before. She introduced Bill to the people she worked for. They were like her family. They took an immediate liking to Bill and felt Katherine had met someone who would be very good to her. The mother of the house encouraged Katherine to marry him. "Don't let him get away…he's a good catch," she would say to Katherine. Katherine didn't have her father for a matchmaker, so this came as close as she could get to having one.

Bill worked at the lumber mill in Boston. He didn't have a car at the time. Their dates consisted of many long walks for ice cream or a bite to eat. Katherine disliked drinking of any kind. Fortunately Bill drank very little. On occasion he would have a beer but never any hard liquor. If they felt extravagant they would take a streetcar.

Bill loved to go to the movies, and this was where he took Katherine on occasion.

Katherine fell in love with Bill. She felt she had met the man of her dreams. Bill knew he wanted to spend the rest of his life with Katherine and asked her to marry him. Katherine said yes. Bill's pet name for Katherine was Katie. Bill and Katherine had dated only three months. It was a short courtship, but Bill was a charmer and had swept Katherine off her feet. Bill knew he had found his "Irish Colleen."

# Chapter III

Roland William Rollins was born on February 25, 1894, in Bangor, Maine. Before he was born, his parents lived in a cabin up in the mountains near a lumber camp. Life presented many hardships during these years. Living in the mountains offered little in the way of luxuries. Water was taken from the river and streams that ran through the mountains. This cool, clear crystal water was used on a daily basis. It provided drinking and cooking water and allowed them to wash their clothes in large tubs with a scrubbing board. In the summer months it was common for women to wash clothes by the streams if weather permitted.

Fuel was provided by chopping down trees and cutting them up for firewood. The firewood was burned in a small potbelly stove to provide heat. The stove was also used for cooking purposes. Kerosene lamps provided the only evening light. It was a lonely and difficult life for a woman. Bill's mother would often walk into town to visit her family and friends. His father was a lumberjack and loved being outdoors. He had many male friends at the lumber camps and would be away from home for several days at a time. Because he was happy being a lumberjack, he wasn't aware of the crude and hard way of life that they lived.

Maine has very cold winters and a great deal of snow. It is not uncommon to have several feet of snow on the ground at one time. This made traveling very difficult. Horses were used for transportation, but the most common way to travel was walking. Winter travel was limited, and trips into town meant you brought back large supplies of food on sleds. The smaller sleds you pulled by hand. Horses would pull the larger sleds up the mountains. There were several trails leading down the mountains into the town. The family cabin was a distance of about five miles from town. In the mountains you had to learn your way around. If you took the wrong trail you would end up in a different lumber camp or worse. You could get lost!

Regardless of this difficult life, the scenery was beautiful. On a warm summer day with clear blue skies one felt as though you could reach up and touch the fluffy white clouds. From the mountaintop you could see the clouds below, above, and all around. What a unique feeling. You felt as though you were a part of the vast universe on a different level. It was a peaceful, quiet, and serene setting. Winter also provided a breathtaking view.

The sun would shine upon the snow, making it glisten like fire.

Bill never knew his mother as she died at his birth. He was their only child. His father didn't have time to devote to young Bill. When he was an infant he was taken into town to be raised by his Aunt Rose (his mother's sister). Bill became very fond of his aunt. He loved her like his own mother, and she was the only mother he ever really knew.

When Bill grew older, his father was remarried to a very young girl. Bill was expected to live with them. This young girl became his stepmother. She wasn't much older than Bill and didn't like him being around. He was an extra mouth to feed and care for. Bill's father and young wife were soon raising a new family of their own. The young wife wanted Bill out of the way. She would make up stories and tell his father lies about him. This caused conflict between Bill and his father. His father would get angry with him, and there was constant friction between them. Occasionally Bill would help his father cut logs and float them down the river. He also helped out at the logging camps where they cut the logs and made them into lumber. The lumber was shipped to large cities. People would buy lumber to build homes and other buildings. Bill found this type of work very hard and didn't want to follow in his father's footsteps.

Bill soon became very resentful toward his father and longed for the day when he would be on his own. As he grew into his pre-teen years, he would walk down from the mountains to spend more time with his aunt. Bill considered his aunt to be his only real family. Bill loved her very much. While living with her, his favorite pastime was going to the movie house. While watching movies he could escape the world he existed in and dream of a life where he was happy and prosperous.

The town of Bangor, Maine, was very small by most standards. If you traveled there today you would see the town in much the same way as it was then. Modern conveniences such as electricity, telephones, cars, and paved streets have naturally developed. Despite the advance of progress, much of the atmosphere remains the same as when young Bill grew up there many years ago. Some of the very old structures that remain give Bangor the feeling that time has stood still. Life there remains very simple compared to current standards.

Bill attended one small elementary school and then the local high school. He loved going to school and was considered to be very smart. He wanted to graduate from high school because he had dreams to fulfill. Eventually he had to quit school in the eleventh grade. Considering the era, that was still considered quite a good education.

Bill went to work in the local movie house because he needed an income. He operated the movie projector for the films. As he sat in the projection booth, he would dream of the day when he could be like a movie hero (Rudolph Valentino was very popular). He wanted to start a life of his own. He rented a room at the boarding house near his aunt's home. At sixteen years of age, Bill was living independently. Bill's childhood was an unhappy one and he longed for the day when he could make a better life for himself. Bill felt his father had deserted him. The time had come for him to try and make his own way in life.

Bill grew up quickly and before his time. When he was only seventeen he began living with a girl his own age. During the first year they lived together they had a set of twins (a boy and a girl). The following year they had another baby girl. Soon Bill felt he was trapped. They were very poor, and most of the time they had nothing to eat. It seemed hopeless. Bill knew if it wasn't for the girl's parents they would starve. He felt he needed to leave and start all over. He wasn't living the kind of life he had dreamed of. He regretted quitting school and wished he had finished his education. Bill desperately longed for a job that would get him the better things in life. He realized it would be difficult to find a good job without an education. Bill was determined to try, but not in Bangor, Maine.

At the age of nineteen, Bill left his small, remote hometown near the mountains and went to live in Boston, Massachusetts. He felt that life in a big city would give him many opportunities to find a better job. Many trades were being taught to men who were willing to learn. Bill was eager to learn. He found a job working in a lumber mill and rented a place nearby to live. Bill knew his downfall was women. He tried hard not to become involved with anyone else for some time. The older he got and the longer Bill was out on his own, the more he realized the importance of an education. He realized that better-paying jobs were available only to those who had a high school diploma. Bill was also feeling guilty about leaving his family in Maine. He knew he had family obligations there. Despite his family in Bangor, Bill never returned to Maine until many years later. Bill carried this guilt with him for the rest of his life.

Because Bill was trying to start a new life, he changed his name from Rollins to Collins. Bill was good-looking and had a wonderful personality. He had a great sense of humor and loved to tease the ladies. He was about five feet and eight inches tall and weighed about 160 pounds. He had strawberry blonde hair and blue eyes. Most everyone called him Bill but sometimes he was called "Red." He was liked by everyone who knew him. Bill loved people and was a great talker. He knew he had a way with words and enjoyed using this talent whenever he could. He especially liked to charm the ladies. Bill had a good eye for what he called the "best-looking ones" and was known to be a ladies' man.

America was in a time of transition. Many new jobs were opening up and required a specific skill. Bill longed to advance to a better position but was unable to find anyone to give him a chance. Bill continued to bide his time and wait for the right opportunity to come his way. A common expression that he would use throughout his lifetime emerged. He was waiting for his "ship to come in."

In Boston, Bill grew older and met another girl. He felt he was ready to take on the responsibility of being a good husband and father. They were married and had two children (a boy and a girl). His wife died when the girl was born. Remembering what his early childhood was like, Bill promised himself he would take care of these children. He wanted his son and daughter to have a better childhood than he did. Bill was unable to do this, and had to put the children in a foster home. Bill paid for their care and would visit them from time to time. When the children were placed in the home, it was understood that they were his children. They were not to be put up for adoption. Bill never signed legal papers to that effect, however. Bill continued working and supporting his children. As time went by, he contacted old friends in Bangor to get news of his other children. He received word that his other children were being well cared for by their mother and grandparents. This gave him some peace of mind knowing they were loved and looked after.

Bill was now thirty years old. He wondered about his life in the future. He missed the closeness of having a wife and children. Bill felt a need for the kind of love that a family brings. He was tired of living alone.

On a beautiful Sunday afternoon in June, he met Katherine at the beach. He felt she was the answer to his dreams. He was entertained by the fact that she was born and raised in Ireland. She was not fully accustomed to American life, and he was amused by her innocence. He fell quickly in love with her and wanted to take care of her the rest of his life. Bill's Aunt Rose had always told Bill that he had Irish blood in him on his mother's side.

Bill was reading in all the newspapers about the automobile factories in Detroit, Michigan. Cars were becoming the main source of transportation in America. They were assembled at the factories in Detroit. Bill understood that jobs were plentiful there and the pay was good. He knew if he was going to get married again he needed better paying work. He discussed this with Katherine, and they decided he should go to Detroit to seek employment. If he found a job he would send for Katherine, and they would get married.

Bill left for Detroit and got a job right away. He was working for the Hudson Motor Car Company. He earned forty cents an hour. This was considered good money at the time. Bill felt he had struck it rich! He sent for Katherine to come to Detroit on a train.

It was fall when Katherine arrived. Bill was there to greet her. They wanted to be married as soon as possible. Katherine felt the need to see a priest that very day. She knew that in America there weren't match makers. They went to a parish priest and discussed marriage arrangements. The priest sensed how uncomfortable Katherine was about living in a strange city and decided to marry them right that very minute. The priest called in his assistant and the housekeeper to witness the ceremony. Katherine and Bill were married September 20, 1924. It was the beginning a new life together in the bustling city of Detroit.

*Author's note: In succeeding chapters, Katherine and Bill will be referred to as Mother and Dad.*

# Chapter IV

Mother and Dad found an apartment to rent in the city of Detroit. It was a third floor walk up. To help with expenses, Mother agreed to maintain the building's furnace. Coal furnaces were used to heat buildings back then. She would go down to the basement throughout the day, the evening, and into the night in order to "stoke" the coals. That was necessary in order to keep the coal fire from going out. This required her to climb up and down three flights of stairs to shovel coal into the furnace morning, noon, and night.

Dad did not want Mother working that hard. He was employed at Hudson's and made good money. He felt Mother had worked all her life and he wanted to take care of her now. Mother, on the other hand, was happy to take on the job in order to fulfill her role as a helpmate to Dad. Despite the hardships, this season in life would be one of her most carefree.

Mother and Dad had dreams of owning their very

own home some day. Mother wanted to start saving as soon as they could. However, she soon found out that Dad was rather frivolous with their money. While his intentions were good, he could not keep a dime in his pocket. Mother, on the other hand, was considered a "saver." Money was very scarce and hard to come by throughout her life. Money was almost a sacred thing to her. You didn't waste money! Dad realized that if they were to get ahead in their marriage, he would have to hand the money over to Mother to manage.

Winter came, and the weather became very cold. Mom had to make more and more trips up and down the stairway to stoke the furnace. Dad became concerned for Mom. He felt it was too much for her. He insisted that when a first-floor apartment opened up, they should take it. Mother protested because first-floor apartments were more costly to rent. She was trying to save every penny she could for a future home of their own. Still, it pleased Mom to know that Dad was so caring and concerned for her welfare. A first-floor apartment soon opened, and they moved downstairs. Mother was quietly thankful that she would no longer have to climb so many stairs to stoke the furnace. Finally, a better night's sleep! Even though Mom was never one to complain about hard work, she was pleased at Dad's thoughtfulness. She kept these treasured memories inside her heart.

Mother realized that Dad had a much better education than she did. This never bothered Dad, but it bothered her.

She vowed to learn as much as she could. Mom spent her leisure time reading and learning about America. She was enjoying her new life and the many things she could learn. She would read newspapers and magazines to keep her informed on current affairs. For the first time Mother was beginning to realize how much an education meant in America. She felt bad that she had only a third-grade education. There was a strong desire to learn as much as she could and keep abreast of what was going on in the world.

Mother was proud of the job Dad had in the automobile factory. Cars were the way of the future, and his job provided them with security. She wanted to learn as much as she could about the auto factories. This was easily accomplished as they lived in Detroit, the capital of the automotive industry.

By the 19th century, lifestyles were beginning to change. There were now warming stoves and furnaces instead of open hearth fireplaces. Homes became more comfortable. Larger windows were installed and sunlight made the rooms brighter. Despite these improvements, Mother began to realize that she was not happy living in the city. Something was missing. It was the open land, grass, trees, and gardens.

Houseplants in America were becoming very fashionable. Ferns were the most fashionable of all. Every well-decorated parlor had a fern or was somehow adorned with greenery. In previous years, homes were too cold and dark for plants to thrive indoors. Mother had learned about indoor houseplants by reading magazines. She became interested in them too. Mom (who wanted to be in style), soon grew many ferns in the apartment. Their apartment became alive with plants in every room. Mother believed she could make anything grow. She was soon recognized as someone with a "green thumb."

Her new hobby was a constant reminder of her love for the land. It helped fill her longing for rural life, but also made her realize how much she truly missed the countryside. She hoped that someday they might have their own home in the country and raise a family together. Mother's nest egg was growing very slowly. She was diligent in putting some money away each week. She hoped it wouldn't take too long to have a down payment on a house. Mother vividly remembered her early life in Ireland. She was aware of the struggle involved in owning a piece of land and being able to keep it.

For their first-year anniversary Dad bought Mom a beautiful white gold watch. He was pleased that he could afford to buy Mom such a lovely piece of jewelry. Mom (who was never one for frills), was upset at the time that he bought it. While she loved the watch very much, she felt the money was wasted on her. The money could have been spent on other things that were needed. It could have been used toward the down payment on their home. Still, Mother's most prized possession throughout her life would be this beautiful white gold watch. She kept it in a green velvet box tied with a ribbon.

In their second year of marriage, Mom became pregnant. They were very happy about this and looked forward to having a baby. They wanted to have the child in their own home. Before the baby was born, they were able to put a small down payment on a home in the city of Detroit. It was located on St. Jean Street.

Mother and Dad bought the usual items for their home, including a dining room set with a sideboard, beds, dressers and a washing machine. Mom had been washing clothes in a tub with a scrub brush. Now she had a new Maytag washing machine. After the clothes were washed, she would take one item at a time and put it through an electric roller to wring out the water. This was a new and modern way of washing clothes. After, the clothes were taken outside and hung on a clothesline to dry. You had to make sure it didn't rain that day! Mother kept that washing machine for years. Constant use literally wore a hole in the tub.

A special purchase was made to help celebrate their move. Dad and Mother bought a rather expensive item for their parlor. It was a chiming mantle clock made by Howard Miller. Dad installed a wooden mantle in the parlor to set the clock on. Once a week you had to wind it with a key. Mother was happy with the clock and enjoyed having it, but Dad was especially thrilled. For him the clock became a symbol of the finer things in life. He hoped it was just the tip of the iceberg, a sign of greater provision for the family in the near future. It represented his belief that someday "his ship" would really come in. The clock became his most prized procession.

The recently purchased house had an upstairs. It was customary to rent out the upstairs (referred to as an upper flat), if you weren't using the space. Mother and Dad decided to rent the upper flat in order to help with the family income. It was customary that if you had a boarder in your home, you supplied them with their meals. Mother was accustomed to cooking, and so she cooked the meals for everyone.

Roland John was their firstborn son. He arrived on March 4, 1926. During the next three years, three more children were born. Catherine was born on May 15, 1927. Andrew was born May 28, 1928. Mary was born during the era of the Great Depression on September 25, 1929.

Mother birthed all these children in their home. She was assisted by a midwife (usually a neighbor woman). Hospitals were very expensive and they didn't have the money for such a luxury. After the delivery of a child, the doctor would make a house call. These visits ensured that Mother and baby were being well cared for.

Caring for a small infant and three young children kept Mom very busy. She had little time for herself. She spent long hours dedicated to ironing, washing, cooking, baking, and cleaning. These were her daily chores, but she was used to hard work.

During this time, Mother had a most unpleasant experience with a childhood disease. It was expected that children would get measles and mumps. Unfortunately, when her children got the mumps, Mom got them too! She never had them as a child and she became very sick. It became difficult for her to continue her daily work. She was rarely in poor health during her lifetime. Other than an occasional cold, she was always very healthy. Mother became so ill that she thought she was going to die. She recalled the severity of this sickness many times throughout her life.

Mother and Dad now had a thriving little family. Dad continued to work for the Hudson Motor Car Company. Mother continued to take in borders. Dad felt their lives were near perfect. They were beginning to have all the things in life he longed for: a wonderful wife, beautiful children, a home of their own, and a good job. Things were going great!

It was during these early years of marriage that Mother's sister, Anna, moved to Detroit too. She fell in love with a young man named Tony. They were soon married. Between the two couples they saved their pennies and sent money back to Ireland in order to bring their brother Mike to America.

Uncle Mike came to the United States and got a job in the country working on a farm. Mom felt very proud that she was eventually able to bring over both her brother and sister from Ireland to the United States. She now had part of her family with her. She knew they would have the opportunity to make a good living. They would be spared the poverty so widespread in Ireland.

During these early years, Mother and Dad enjoyed their little family. As the family began to grow, America experienced many growing pains as well. There were many changes on the horizon.

Education took on a new look in American school buildings. They became much larger than they were in the past. The one-room schoolhouse was disappearing. Secondary education was becoming a necessity, as many jobs now required a high school diploma. A new way to finance schools evolved and taxes were imposed. Teacher salaries increased and central schools became the norm. An expanded curriculum including many new subject areas were included. Bussing became necessary as schools became more centralized and students needed a means of transportation to and from their homes. Graduating high school seniors considered college to be a more common and viable option.

America also experienced many challenges on the economic and political scene. During the 1920s, three major technological industries were booming. These included the automobile, radio, and "talking" movies (the transition from silent films).

Despite this growth, the economy was struggling. World War I left America heavily in debt. The debt put additional tax burdens on the people and clogged international trade. Agriculture was also suffering due to high freight charges, low wages, and increased taxes. Farm equipment and supplies were highly priced. People had to buy less even though the markets were producing more. Soon there was an overproduction of goods that hurt the economy.

Economic conditions continued to decline until the stock market eventually crashed in September of 1929. The government did not have internal safe guards to protect banking investments. By mid November, investors had lost 30 billion dollars. Due to the ravaged economy, President Coolidge chose not to run a second term as President of the United States. Herbert Hoover became the new president in 1928. He was unable to stop the economic devastation. It would take twelve long years for America to recover from this Great Depression.

As America worked through these troubled times, Mother and Dad continued to live their lives confronting personal challenges of their own. Mother had meaningful family ties and was concerned that Dad had such a strong dislike for his father. She felt a trip back east was in order. She was certain Dad's father would want to see him again and would want to know about his grandchildren. Mom wanted this to be a chance for reconciliation between Dad and his father. Dad didn't want to go. He was sure that his father really didn't care about him or his life. Mother just wouldn't believe that. She had such a wonderful relationship with her own father. Mom missed her dad dearly, and she couldn't imagine a father figure that could be so uncaring.

An old Ford was purchased to make the drive from

Michigan to Maine. Mother would pack lunches to keep down the cost of food. In the summer of 1930 they left Detroit with their four children and headed east.

Things did not go well from the start. It was very hot in the car and the children were very restless. Mary was just a baby and cried a lot. It took several days to get there, and everyone's patience was frazzled. To make matters worse, Mom didn't like the big mountains of Maine. She was familiar with the rolling hills of Ireland, but not such big mountains! Mother became very nervous and got sick. To make matters even worse, the car kept overheating going up the steep mountains. Dad had to keep stopping in order to allow the engine to cool down.

Finally they arrived. Mother's relief was short-lived. Dad's father showed no interest in their being there! They stayed for a short period of time and left. Mother was very perplexed and sad for everyone involved. They had traveled so far. This was such a wasted opportunity. Dad's father really didn't care. While this shocked Mother, it came as no surprise to Dad. He hadn't expected anything from his dad and wasn't disappointed. He was just happy to get his family back home to Detroit.

During the Depression years, Mother and Dad were concerned about feeding their little family and paying their bills. The automobile factories suffered terribly because no one had money to buy cars. Dad was lucky to make a dollar or two per week. To make up for lost work he took a part-time job selling real estate. Of course people were not buying homes either, but Dad tried desperately to make a few extra dollars.

As the stock market crashed, large numbers of factory workers were laid off. They had no income and many were going hungry. Businesses failed, stores were closing, banks were going broke, and the future looked bleak. With many people losing thousands of dollars from bank failures and failing markets, some people became incredibly desperate. Suicide became a tragic response to their loss and many jumped out the windows of tall buildings, falling to their deaths.

Mother was terrified as these events unfolded. They reminded her of the suffering and hunger that had taken place in Ireland. She felt a greater need now to acquire land. If they owned their own land they could at least grow vegetables in order to help feed the family. Mother and Dad started their search for land away from the city of Detroit.

In 1931 the family moved north of Detroit to Harrison Township. This was near Mount Clemens. They bought five acres of vacant land on a street named Longview, just off South River Road. Even though Dad had no experience building houses, he built a house for his family. Dad would draw upon his childhood in Maine. He was not a carpenter, but had always worked with lumber at the saw mills. He had a strong sense of what needed to be done and accomplished it. The house had very crude lighting, no water or plumbing, and an outdoor bathroom (outhouse).

Dad and Rose

The summer of 1933—The first house Dad constructed

*Rose Marie Rivard*

Dad drove his old car back and forth to work in Detroit. When the car broke down, Dad had to learn how to fix it. There was no money to pay a mechanic. He had to learn many things he had never done before. Soon he considered himself a "jack of all trades and master of none." This became an often-quoted expression of his.

In 1932 I became part of the Collins family. Mother had her fifth child. I was their newest baby girl. Dad wanted to name me Rose, after his favorite aunt in Maine. Dad had fond memories of his Aunt Rose, and I would be named in remembrance of her. Mother agreed. Throughout the years this caused substantial sibling rivalry. My brothers and sisters felt I became Dad's favorite in the family. Some would say I was the "apple of Daddy's eye."

By 1932, the American economy was near rock bottom. In large cities like Detroit it was not uncommon to see bread lines. There were also soup kitchens and street vendors who tried to sell apples for pennies on the street corners. It was a very difficult time. People struggled to get the very basics for survival. Many were so hungry they searched through garbage containers in order to gather food. A song popularized in that era was, "Brother, Can You Spare a Dime?"

On the political scene, the people blamed President Hoover for the Great Depression. He was defeated in the next election. President Roosevelt was elected in 1932. He promised the people a "New Deal" to move America forward. Roosevelt utilized the radio in order to conduct what became known as "fireside chats." The American people listened to his talks. These radio broadcasts made him so popular that the American people elected him to the presidency four times. Many people felt Roosevelt was a tremendous leader. President Roosevelt believed that he could only lead the people in a direction they wanted to go.

Back on the home front, Mother and Dad were discovering the advantages and disadvantages of country living. Mom began feeling very isolated. She had no way to get out and about. Mother and Dad decided they needed another automobile (even though Mother had not yet learned how to drive). After Dad purchased their second vehicle, Mom would take the old car out for a drive. It was summertime and she would practice driving around the empty fields near our home. With great laughter, she would recall many years later how her neighbor reacted to her learning to drive. When he was working in his garden and saw her at the wheel, he would grab his hoe and run for the house!

Once Mother learned to drive she was able to take the older children to school. There weren't any schools located near our home, and Mom decided to send the children to St. Louis Catholic School on the outskirts of Mount Clemens. This was about a five-mile drive. Mom recalled that she would never pass up a child who needed a ride to school. She would "pack them in" as she was fond of saying. I was too little to attend school, but the four older children attended regularly.

Mother worked very hard putting in a garden in order to keep food on the table. Unfortunately, Mother and Dad discovered that their little plot of ground tended to be located in a low area. The soil was often very wet and soggy. The land was located near the Clinton River and was subject to frequent flooding. Mother also learned very quickly that unlike Ireland (which had a long growing season), the Michigan agricultural season was very short. Because of the short growing season, canning food was a popular thing to do. This would allow you to store various kinds of food in preparation for the long winter months. Mother had never canned food before, but she was willing to learn if it would help feed the family.

An additional enduring family hardship was the lack of well water. After several attempts, Dad was never successful at getting anything other than surface water in the well. Mother gathered large milk cans and bought large glass water jugs. She then drove to the water plant to secure drinking and cooking water. It became necessary to do this several times a week.

Living conditions were hard, and Mom continued to struggle with her gardening efforts. She acquired all the canning supplies needed, and soon her attempts to can fruit and vegetables were successful. With a second car and her new driving skills, she regularly made the water runs and transported the children to school.

Dad began to experience the effects of country living in Michigan. His eyes became itchy and red in the fall season. They would water and there were times when he would have difficulty breathing. One night Dad's eyes became so irritated that he got up to get some water. As he was going into the kitchen, he tripped and fell over one of the toys lying on the floor. He became very angry and started using some "colorful language." Mom scolded him for this. This was the first time I ever heard Mother scold Dad for his language, but not the last. Later, Mom took Dad to see a doctor. He was told he had an allergy commonly known as "hay fever." Dad would suffer with this allergy the rest of his life. In later years they would escape the allergy season by traveling up north or going south to Florida. It seemed the only way to find relief from the ragweed pollen.

Aunt Anna and Uncle Tony had been living in Detroit with their three small children. They decided to leave the city and move near Mother and Dad in Harrison Township. Mom enjoyed having her sister Anna living close by. This was a great comfort to her. They lived on the next street over from our family. They would visit often. Mother enjoyed their company, but Aunt Anna and Uncle Tony did not enjoy the living conditions in the countryside. They didn't live near us for long and soon moved back to Detroit.

One day Mom bumped her ankle and broke a blood vessel. She was devastated as the doctor told her she would have to stay completely off her feet for six weeks. She didn't know how she was going to care for her family. I was three years old when she showed me how to make a "train of chairs." Mom used the train of chairs by sliding across them to get from room to room. The neighbors pitched in and helped get the older children to and from school. With great difficulty, Mother managed to cook and care for the family.

Mother remembered another difficult time when all five of us got the measles. We were all sick within days of each other. Mother was told by the doctor to keep us in dark rooms to protect our vision. It was believed at that time you could go blind from the measles if you were exposed to light. We had to avoid the sunlight. Our rooms were kept dark during the day by hanging blankets over the windows. As the youngest, I didn't understand any of this. Staying in a dark room all day seemed strange and unfamiliar. It made me afraid. I remained afraid of the dark until my teen years.

One year I received a beautiful ring for my birthday. It was given to me by my godfather. He was a neighbor that lived nearby on the next street. That ring meant a lot to me. I wore the ring one summer day while in the garden with Mother. I lost the ring in the garden and was very upset. Mom knew how much the ring meant to me. We spent part of afternoon in the garden digging in the soil looking for it. Mother scolded me for wearing it outdoors. I was told that jewelry was not to be worn when working but only for pleasure.

Times were hard for Mother and Dad. There were five children to feed and provide for. Dad's work at the factory was very slow. To save on expenses, Mother bought a sewing machine and taught herself to make clothes for the family. They were not fancy, but she would repeat what her father had said to them as children. She remembered, "If you have food on the table, clothes on your back, and a roof over your head, you should be thankful." Dad bought used shoe repair equipment and repaired all our shoes. This helped to keep down expenses too. It seemed like we were always in need of shoes and clothing. Clothes were handed down from one child to the next. Over the years I know I got my fair share of hand-me-down clothes!

Mom baked all the bread and biscuits. Cookies were rare because they were treats. Not necessary to "fill the stomach," as Mother would often say. She always made birthday cakes for us, though, and everyone looked forward to having a piece of cake. Mother and Dad rarely went into town. When we needed supplies, Mother would buy a few groceries at a small country store.

Dad would often take me with him on Saturday mornings to a junk yard on the edge of the riverfront. There was a little, old shack that sat ever so picturesque on the bank of the Clinton River. It was surrounded by tall trees and green grass. I recall the man who owned it.

He was very proud of his little store. He even kept the junk yard very clean and neat, unlike what you would think a junk place to be. He was a very old man with a long, gray beard. He was always happy to see me. I remember his compliments as he often told me what a pretty little girl I was. Dad would buy tools or equipment that he needed to fix things. I loved going on these trips with my dad. We were building a very special bond and it lasted a lifetime. I always felt happy and special when we were together. I never really realized at the time that we were a poor family. Such is the innocence of a child.

It was rare that all the family went to town together. I recall one event when we went together to the 5 & 10 cent store. It was in the fall, and Mother needed to buy supplies for the older children to go back to school. Dad took all of us to see the candy counter. I was amazed to see so much candy in one place. Everything looked good. Unbeknown to Mom, Dad bought some penny candy. When Mom finished shopping we left for home. Mother noticed everyone was eating candy. She sternly looked at Dad and said, "You're wasting money on things we can't afford." Mother knew that Dad had a big sweet tooth though and that he enjoyed the candy as much as we did!

Driving home, it soon became dark. The moon came out shining brightly. It reflected across the water on the river. It looked so beautiful. My brothers and sisters sat in the back seat of the Model T Ford. They were happily eating their candy. I sat snuggled between Mom and Dad in the front seat. Mother was quietly humming a song to herself that evening. She seemed so happy and content. She worked so hard that I didn't often see her this way. She was frequently tired and restrained. I have treasured this memory throughout my life. I can still picture the scene of Mother and Dad driving us home along the beautiful moonlit riverfront that night.

Catherine, Rose, Mary, Andy, Roland
Summer of 1935

# Chapter V

The year was now 1936. Mother once again felt the need to purchase more land. The goal was to expand the farm beyond the growing of just a few vegetables. Dad didn't consider himself to be a farmer, but was willing to give it a try in order to feed his family. With Mother's help, they would try to make it work. Along with his newfound skills in cement work, wiring, and house building, Dad would learn how to farm. Mother taught him how to milk a cow, harness a horse, plow a field, and plant a crop. Dad continued his job at the auto factory, which was now only part time. He felt his dreams of living a grander lifestyle were slipping away. He wondered if his ship would ever come in.

Mother and Dad purchased an eighty-acre farm in the Richmond area on 32 Mile Road. The house and other buildings sat back from the road. It had a long, curved driveway that led to a tall, narrow, and very old farmhouse. This would become our new home. The house was a dull, weather-beaten, gray color. It was in obvious need of paint and repairs. The house was surrounded by large, tall trees. Behind the house was a large barn and shed. The farm was so far out in the country that there wasn't any electric power at that time. As the farmhouse didn't have electricity, kerosene lamps were used for lighting. There was an outside well. We carried water into the house with buckets. The water was used for drinking, cooking, and washing. Mother was grateful for the outdoor well. It made things a little easier for her.

The bathroom consisted of an outdoor toilet. This was a relatively common circumstance in rural areas during the mid 1930s. The downstairs had a living room, dining room, and kitchen. The kitchen had cupboards, countertops, and an old iron stove used for cooking and baking. There were three large bedrooms upstairs. The stairway leading up to the bedrooms was very dark, narrow, and steep. Mother was afraid that I would fall down the stairs. She insisted I scoot down the stairway on my butt. Eventually I became afraid of the stairway, picking up on the worry in Mom's voice about falling.

For heat we had a large pot-bellied stove in the dining room. The stovepipe chimney went through the upstairs area and ventilated out the roof. The stovepipe gave off a little heat for the upstairs bedrooms (very little). This was the only source of heat in the winter months, and we complained about getting dressed for school during cold winter mornings.

Mother would rise about 4:30 a.m. She would stoke the stove and rekindle a fire to warm the old house. Dad's breakfast would be prepared, and she would pack his lunch. After seeing him off to work, she began doing the outside chores with the help of the older children. Once again inside, she would prepare breakfast for the children and pack their school lunches. It was so cold on many early winter mornings that it was not uncommon to find ice in the water buckets inside our kitchen.

Mother and Dad always moved their furniture with them from house to house. There wasn't a place to put the cherished mantle clock, so it was kept on the sideboard. Dad wanted to put up a shelf but was afraid with one pound of the hammer the plaster would come tumbling down. There were already many cracks in the plaster as it was.

Mom couldn't use her washing machine because there wasn't any electricity. She had to go back to washing clothes with a wash tub and scrubbing board. While things were difficult, Mom never complained. She always thanked God for His many blessings.

The land in Richmond had rich black soil that would yield good crops. Mother and Dad soon purchased a horse that would help plow up the ground. The planting area was too much for one horse, and a second horse was needed to make a team.

Mother and Dad bought baby chickens and ducks from the Sears and Roebuck catalog. They were shipped by mail in large cardboard boxes with peek holes in the sides (for air and ventilation). It was exciting to see this very special delivery. Yellow baby chickens and tiny ducks! How the mailman ever felt about the noise in his car with all those little critters would be another story. As children, we loved to see them arrive! Mom also raised and sold turkeys. They were a popular item around the holidays.

Mother and Dad bought a cow for cream and milk. With the cream, Mom was able to make fresh butter. I remember helping her make the fresh butter. We took nearly a gallon of cream (slightly souring) and put it in a large openmouthed jug. The jug was then shaken (for what seemed to be hours). Mom and I took turns shaking the jug. I felt my arms would fall off! I was actually too little to be of much help at the time. Because she always seemed to be doing nothing but work, I felt I needed to help as best I could. Eventually the cream would separate into particles of butter. The particles would stick together to form a ball. The ball was taken out of the jug, and the result was fresh butter. The remaining liquid was buttermilk. Mom loved to drink fresh buttermilk! She tried to tell her sons and daughters how good it was, but none of us seemed to be able to acquire a taste for it.

Roland was old enough to help Dad or Mother get the horses ready for plowing in the spring. Everyone helped to plant and weed. In the summer months the farm did produce bountiful crops. Mother and the children would work for hours weeding. I remember being scolded for pulling up the little green carrot stems that I thought were weeds! After that, Mother didn't want me in the garden. She said I was too little, but I had nothing else to do and wanted to help.

Strawberries grew wild in the fields in the springtime. We would pick them for Mom, and she would make fresh strawberry jam. She also made grape jam from grapes that were purchased at the local store. After the summer crops were harvested, Mom spent hours in the kitchen canning vegetables. It was not uncommon for her to can more than one hundred jars in the fall. All these things kept us well supplied during the winter months.

Because we lived on a farm, there was always a variety of things to eat. Along with the potatoes and vegetables there were fresh eggs, milk, and butter. Baked bread was always fresh out of the oven, as were homemade biscuits. When in season there were always fresh fruit and vegetables on the table. During the off seasons there was always an amply stocked variety of canned goods and jellies. Mother showed us how to make a dirt cellar for the root vegetables.

For special treats, I remember Mom learned to make homemade mincemeat pies. They were a very special holiday treat. During the hot summer months she would make root beer from a powder mixture supplied from the Watkins delivery truck. The Watkins truck went door to door in those days, selling their merchandise. On a rare occasion Mother would buy strawberry pop. She allowed herself few treats, but strawberry pop was one of her favorites, and she shared it with us!

As a child, I remember my stomach was occasionally upset, and I sometimes needed to vomit. This was concerning, but we couldn't figure out what caused the upset. Doctors were expensive and the family didn't go often. One day Dad took me to see the doctor, but he too was unable to find anything wrong. My illness remained a mystery for years. Decades later when I was married with children, my husband and I went on a vacation to see Mother and Dad. Mom had strawberry pop in her refrigerator and invited me to have some. That night I became seriously ill. It was then that I realized I was allergic to the red dye in strawberry pop. That solved the mystery of my childhood illness. To this day I need to be careful to avoid that type of red dye.

Mother also learned how to make crock dill pickles. She would put dill in with the pickles for processing. If you were anywhere near the big crock, it would beckon you to come and taste! The smell of dill is delightful. We loved to snack on them throughout the day, and Mom felt she couldn't produce enough of them. We ate them as fast as she could make them.

Soon we bought more cows so we could sell their calves. This added to our income. We also bought and sold pigs. Now and then Mother and Dad would butcher a cow or a pig. It is unclear how Mother and Dad ever taught themselves how to butcher meat. Perhaps a neighboring farmer helped them. Dad built a smokehouse to smoke the hams and bacon. I can still remember the aroma that came from the smokehouse. It was wonderful. I still enjoy the smell of any kind of smoked meat.

Mother must have felt she was reliving her life in Ireland. These were the same kinds of things she did as a child and they made many memories.

Dad was making very little money at the Hudson Car company. The country was still experiencing the effects of the depression. In the summer Dad would load up the car with fresh vegetables and eggs and drive to Detroit. Roland and Andrew would go with him, and they would try to sell the farm produce. They traveled to the areas of Detroit where we used to live, hoping that some of the old neighbors would buy our farm goods. Often he returned home late at night with the car still full, having sold only a few cents worth. In those days a large bushel basket of sweet corn sold for 25 cents. Dad was very concerned about our income. Mother always reassured Dad that we would be fine. We had a good supply of food from the farm. We would not go hungry.

The farm provided well for the family. We had chicken for dinner almost every Sunday. Mother would go out into the barnyard and pick out a fat chicken for dinner. As a child in Ireland she had learned to break the chicken's neck, place the chicken in hot scalding water, and then pluck its feathers. She applied these same skills when preparing our meal. On different occasions (because of Dad's eastern/Boston heritage), Mother made a point of making homemade baked beans with fresh cornbread. This was Dad's favorite!

Blueberries were one of Dad's special breakfast treats. In the mountains of Maine, Dad would pick blueberries to eat. He really enjoyed having blueberries on a large stack of flapjacks (pancakes). Blueberries were his favorite fruit. Dad had also learned that you can get syrup from maple trees. He remembered how much he liked eating flapjacks and maple syrup for breakfast when working in the lumber camps in Maine.

In the woods on our farm there were maple trees. Dad began making little maple syrup "taps" whittled from pieces of wood. These homemade taps had a notch that would hold a pail. In the spring, Dad tapped the maple trees in the woods. He inserted these little objects into the tree in order to gather the syrup. It would drip from the tree into the pail. After about a week or so, Dad would check his pails to see how much syrup he collected. Using a home-built sled/wagon, Dad took the horses and pulled the sled through the woods. He went from tree to tree collecting the pails of syrup. I tried to go everywhere my dad did and usually accompanied him on the sled during these journeys. Often there was still snow on the ground, and I enjoyed our many rides together. This was a very happy time for both of us.

I loved the gentle, kind, loving person that Dad was. He was very happy when the family would do things together. It seemed like the hardships of life disappeared during those times. Dad loved his children dearly and would sing "little ditties" to us. He would bounce the smaller children on his knee and sing us silly songs. The older children felt I got most of his attention. Dad loved to play the harmonica and wanted the children to do little dances while he played for us. He loved giving us hugs and kisses, and sat us on his lap. He was forever holding me because I was the smallest. I idolized my father and followed him everywhere he went. Mother was often so busy that she never took the time or the energy for such outward affection. I missed that from her.

Another way Mother saved money was by giving Dad and the boys their own haircuts. She bought a pair of clippers and just started cutting. She had no experience at doing this but learned rather quickly. Those first few haircuts were probably pretty rough, but Dad hung in there. As the boys got older, they went to the barber for "a real haircut," but Dad never went to a barber again in his life.

One day Dad planned to go to Detroit to look for a different job. As the older children were in school, he wanted Mom and me to go with him. Usually Dad made these trips alone. Today he thought it would be a nice change of pace for Mom to get away from her work. Mother always made sure Dad would look proper. She starched and ironed his shirt and pressed his pants so that there were no wrinkles. Off we went to the big city.

I had never seen Detroit before, and asked Mother many, many questions. Dad went inside a large building. I wondered why the buildings were so big. What kind of jobs did people have in those buildings? Why were the people so dressed up? Why did the cars in Detroit come in pretty colors, while our family cars were plain old black? What did the women have on their faces that made them so colorful? Finally, Mother told me to be quiet for awhile. I was asking too many questions. I did learn a lot that day. I began to understand that not everyone lived the same way we did. Were we poor?

Over the years, we sometimes asked Mother about being poor. She always said we were not poor because "we have a roof over our heads, clothes on our backs, and food on the table." She wanted us to thank God for the many things we did have. Dad always kept silent on the matter. Perhaps he wanted to admit to our poverty and really agreed more with us than Mom on that topic.

When Dad would come back from his job-searching trips, he always looked forlorn and tired. He was turned away from the jobs he wanted because he didn't have a high school diploma. It was becoming apparent that there were two types of work, skilled and unskilled. Dad hated being considered unskilled. Through the years Dad and Mother would often talk to us about how important it was to get a good education. They wanted us to "amount to something" and hoped their children would become educated in order to avoid unskilled jobs like "digging ditches."

After Mother and Dad were on the farm for about two years, I was old enough to start school. I went to a one-room schoolhouse a few miles from the farm. To me it seemed a long way, and I didn't like being so far from home. It was also a very long walk. I had a male teacher, and I didn't like him. The teacher told Mother that I cried a lot and would fall asleep. Mother felt I was too young for school. As a result I was able to skip kindergarten. Only first grade was required.

School buses didn't exist yet. Usually you had to walk to school. It was not uncommon to walk five or six miles to school, then walk back home again at the end of the day. It didn't matter if it was raining or snowing. Occasionally some school teachers would remove the seats from their cars and replace them with wooden benches. The teacher would drive around the area picking up as many children as they could. Most of the time, however, you had to walk to school.

My siblings did their homework right after they got home from school. It was difficult to see at night because we only had a kerosene lamp for light. To protect eyesight, Mother encouraged them to finish their schoolwork before dusk. I remember watching my father and mother trying to read the newspaper after dark, and it was very difficult with the low glow of a kerosene lamp.

Our second car from Harrison never made the move

to Richmond. Mother felt we needed to replace it. Dad always bought Ford cars because they were the cheapest, even when brand new. Ford took pride in making a "working man's car." Dad brought home a used Ford with a rumble seat. We loved the car with the rumble seat, and everyone wanted to ride in it! Mother wasn't thrilled, but we were. I wanted to ride in the rumble seat too, but Mother and Dad felt that I was too little and might fall out. I was disappointed about that.

One Sunday Mother got all of us dressed in our nicest clothes for church. Dad came over to the car to say good-bye. Dad was not Catholic at that time and didn't go to church. As Mom closed the car door, she didn't realize Dad's hand was still on the edge of the door when she slammed it. The door ripped open his finger and tore off his fingernail. Dad was in great pain, and his hand was bleeding badly. Mother hurried to care for his hand. No one made it to church that Sunday, and Dad's fingernail remained scarred for the rest of his life. As we grew older, we often asked Dad why he never helped Mom out around the kitchen. Now his standard answer was, "I can't, I have a sore finger."

Mom and Dad stayed on the farm in Richmond for about three years. The old farmhouse was so tall that Mother felt the house sway during strong winds and thunderstorms. If the storms were especially bad, she would take the children outside. There was an old abandoned car parked behind the barn. We would often take shelter in that old car. Many of the bad storms seemed to happen in the springtime when the older children were in school. Mom and I were the only ones home, so we fled to our shelter. To pass the time until the storm ended, Mom would sing songs and tell nursery rhymes.

Sometimes Mother brought a lunch while we took cover in the old car. I remember an unusual snack consisting of broken pieces of homemade bread mixed with milk and sugar. This was also a common bedtime snack. In the summer it was made with cold milk and in the winter she would warm the milk. Those moments that found the two of us hidden away in the car and safe from the storms were unique. These were some of the few times that I was able to be alone with her. Usually she was busy doing house and farm work. Mother was ill at ease in the house when the storms would rage. She didn't like living there.

Mother, Aunt Anna, and Uncle Mike saved what money they could in order to bring their sister Margaret to America. When she arrived, Mother and Dad had a big family reunion at the farm in Richmond. There was singing and dancing. Mother sang "Danny Boy," a song that she sang many times over the years. It was a very special time and brings back happy memories. Dad felt bad for Mom because she worked for hours getting all the food ready to feed everyone. Mother didn't complain and was happy to have everyone at this special reunion.

Parties were rare, but there were a few that followed throughout the years. Sometimes they would take place at Aunt Anna and Uncle Tony's house in Detroit. I loved to listen to the Irish music and watch the adults dance the Irish jigs.

Looking back over these early years in Richmond, I realize the special bonds that were formed through these family events. Times were hard and money was scarce, but something special was nurtured. It was the love of family.

# Chapter VI

Our family moved into the Chesterfield area on Fairchild Road in the summer of 1938. Dad was happy to move because he felt he was too far from work and hoped to find a steadier job. Now closer to a city, that might be possible.

Mother and Dad bought ten acres of vacant land. The land was located right next door to a one-room schoolhouse. Dad and the boys began building a home. The house had a living room, dining room, kitchen, and three bedrooms (one downstairs and two upstairs). We moved in when the house wasn't completely finished. Dad originally planned an inside bathroom, but that would have to wait. Meanwhile, we had the outhouse.

In the living room, Dad built a fake fireplace to put the mantle clock on. It looked great! Mom seemed concerned that Dad was too attached to that clock. I think Dad considered the clock a symbol. It represented the many nice things that he wanted to provide for us. The clock helped him consider time passing as he "waited for his ship to come in." For Mother it was just a clock. It wasn't working anymore, and she told Dad that he made too much of a fuss over it.

Our furniture was getting old, but it was still useable. Dad wired the house for electricity, and we were able to use indoor lamps and a radio. How great that was! Once again Mother and Dad could listen each week to the President's "fireside chats." They could even read the evening newspaper without eyestrain. We could do our homework later in the evening. Within a few years we would even have a telephone in the house. Imagine that!

Mother was now able to use the electric washing machine again. Dad brought in water from the outside well and set up a small pump by the sink. This made things easier for everyone who helped in the kitchen. Water was still heated on the stove. Dad bought a new electric stove for cooking, baking, and to heat the water. He also put in a coal-burning furnace in the basement.

The stairways leading up to the bedrooms were not steep or very long, as it was a standard two-story house. Mother still loved her plants and grew many of them by the window on a table in the dining room. Everyone felt we were living in the lap of luxury. These were the things Dad wanted for his family, and he felt they were getting ahead in the world. These modern conveniences made life much easier for all, but especially Mom.

Dad built a large shed for the livestock, chickens, and

turkeys. He bought a used tractor for plowing the big garden they planned. Mom would still have to do a lot of canning to see us through the long winter season.

Money continued to be scarce. Dad worked only a few days a week at the auto factory. He felt he was getting really good at building houses, and that sparked an idea. He knew a friend that owned land on North Avenue. They worked out a deal where he would build and sell houses on his friend's land. They would then share the profits from the sale. Dad did this for the next couple of years, and it helped their financial situation considerably. When Roland and Andy were not in school, they were able to help with these building projects as well.

Before moving to Chesterfield, Mother found out she was going to have another baby. Jerome (Jerry) Collins was born January 8, 1939. Mother had this baby in a hospital! While she was away we missed her very much. I remember a neighbor woman who would come in each day to look out after us. Needless to say we were all very excited to get Mom home again and to see the new baby.

In the spring of 1939, Mother found out a neighbor was looking for children to help pick his large field of strawberries. She sent the four older children to work. They would pick berries all day for a penny a quart. They would give the money to Mother. I wanted to help out too. After much pleading, Mother and Dad let me go with my older brothers and sisters. Roland and Catherine didn't want me to go and felt I would be a bother. They didn't want to have to watch over me. At the end of the day, Dad came to pick us up. He asked the farmer how I did. The farmer said that I ate more than I picked! That ended my high-finance career as a strawberry picker.

Life was filled with work for Mother and Dad. Time spent with children was sparse. Mom's days were filled with washing, cooking, canning, baking, sewing, and doing farm chores. She was able to spend a little less time making children's clothes (as they were now able to buy a few things at the 5 & 10 cent store). Mom worked tirelessly and sometimes seemed irritated with Dad. Dad would take time in the midst of the day to play with us. The younger children would be bounced on his knee, and he would sing us silly songs. Mother felt she needed to be stern, and she considered Dad a bit indulgent and tender-hearted. She often told Dad that someone had to be in charge.

During the summer, Dad enjoyed playing baseball with us on Sunday afternoons. Dad kept me near him so he could protect me while he pitched. I was too little to play ball with the older children. One day Roland hit a line drive right at me. The ball hit me in the stomach and knocked the breath out of me! After that Dad put me way out in the outfield so I wouldn't get hurt.

While Mom seemed less affectionate, she did seem extra fond of Roland. Even Dad would agree with the rest of us on that matter. Mother always denied it. In retrospect, I believe Roland reminded Mother of her father. She said that Roland's physical appearance looked like her side of the family. Roland would soon share much of her attention with Jerry. Mother was passing her childbearing years and as the youngest child, Jerry, held a special significance.

Mom and Dad now had six children. You can imagine that there was significant sibling rivalry between us and plenty of opportunity for disagreement. My brothers seemed less competitive. Jerry took the brunt of a lot of teasing, but generally the boys got along well. There always seemed to be more competition amongst my sisters and me. As a little girl my oldest sister and I seemed to have a caring relationship, but over time that would change. My other sister and I developed different personalities and rarely saw eye to eye.

Mother would often warn us about the evils of jealousy. She referred to it as the green-eyed monster. She knew "no good will come from it," and that jealousy would only cause pain. I think she realized early on that jealousy could be the source for future problems in the family. I was happy being the "apple of my father's eye," and totally missed the warning. At that age I never connected the dots.

Back Row Left to Right: Catherine, Roland, Andy
Front Row Left to Right: Rose, Mary
Summer of 1940

For second grade, I began attending the one-room schoolhouse next door to our house. Every year there was a Christmas program. One year I was asked to sing solo. It was a part of the verse from "White Christmas." Mom and Dad were very proud of me. They both beamed when they found out I was chosen. Mom felt I had inherited her singing voice. Mother decided I needed something special to wear that night. Usually my clothes were "hand me downs" from my sisters. Those clothes really didn't fit properly, and most of the time that didn't seem to matter. For Christmas it was customary that we receive clothes and one toy. Mother bought me a beautiful red sweater to wear for the play. That year I got to open one Christmas gift ahead of time!

When I was in third grade, Roland started high school. Mother decided to enroll all of us in St. Mary's Catholic School, Mt. Clemens. Roland could drive by then, and he provided our transportation. Mother felt this would help us with our religious education instead of just having catechism classes on Sunday morning.

I was not happy at St. Mary's. My classmates would tease me about my clothes. I became the target for many taunts, and the names they called me were very cruel. I frequently came home in tears. Mother had many old sayings she would try to comfort us with. One of her most frequent was "sticks and stones may break your bones, but names will never hurt you." Indeed they never hurt physically, but the emotional wounds were very deep.

The nuns would take "needy children" and walk them over to the Salvation Army for a free lunch. They wanted Mother to sign me up for that program. Soon everyone in the class knew I was going. Those of us considered "needy" were ridiculed. I was teased unmercifully by my peers and felt helpless. I begged Mom to get me out of the free lunch program, even if it meant I only had a piece of bread to eat. After many tears and much pleading, Mom let me drop out of the program.

Growing up in the midst of these experiences was difficult. While there was little money to go around during these years, Mother and Dad taught us many values. I learned to work hard, be honest, and never dishonor the family name. They instilled within me a drive to never give up even when the going was rough. Dad taught me to be caring, gentle, and loving. These ideals and family values were special gifts that the Collins' children were exposed to throughout our early lives.

One evening Dad was going to the neighborhood store, and, of course, I went with him. The store had large baskets of freshly picked apples sitting on the floor. I took one and put it in my pocket. I just couldn't resist that large, juicy, red one. On the way home I took the apple out of my pocket. I was about to eat it when Dad asked, "Where did you get that"? I told him. Dad scolded me and took me back to the store. He made me tell the owner that I took his apple, and then I returned it to him. On the way home I was embarrassed and broken-hearted. I never forgot the lesson Dad taught me that night. I was sad that I had disappointed Dad. It was a valuable lesson. I was determined to never again take anything that belonged to someone else. As trying as it was for me to learn the lesson, I believe it was equally difficult for Dad to teach it to me. Dad never brought up the incident again. That was the only time I ever remember him correcting me.

Mother was not one to provide praise for any of her children. She often quipped "we would pass if the crowd is big," which was her way of saying that we were "average" looking. Mother never wanted any of us to think we were pretty or handsome. She was afraid that we might become conceited or boastful.

Mother's faith in God never ceased. She believed in raising her children with good, old-fashioned values. She knew one day she would be accountable to God for what she taught us and how we were raised.

Before bedtime one night on Mother's Day weekend, I tried to tell my older sisters about what I had learned in school that day. A nun had explained how beautiful heaven was. I tried to explain the lesson about heaven. There would be no pain or sorrow, only happiness and joy. The nun had made it sound so beautiful. The nun told us that we should pray for our mothers so that they would go to heaven when they die. My sisters acted shocked, and suggested that I wanted Mom dead! They started to poke fun and say mean things. They threatened to tell Mom that I wanted her dead. I was very hurt and upset. I cried softly so my sisters wouldn't hear. We all slept in the same room, and I didn't want any more of their abuse! I could never understand how I could have been so misunderstood. It was such a beautiful story about heaven, and they totally misunderstood it. Or did they?

Dad would often run errands in town on Saturday mornings. I usually went with him, and we would stop at a little restaurant for pancakes and sausage. Mother only gave Dad a little bit of money at a time, so Dad didn't always have enough money for two breakfasts. I would sit alongside of him, and he would share his pancakes with me. Dad always asked for blueberries, but they never had any. This was one of Dad's favorite breakfasts. He liked eggs, but he had them all the time at home. Mother rarely made pancakes because it took so long to make so many!

I sometimes noticed that Mother would send me out to the garden to call Dad in for supper. He was always hungry after a hard day's work and usually ready to eat. But on occasion, Dad would remain outside hoeing. I wondered why Mom didn't just call him. Why did she always send me? It took awhile before I figured out that on these occasions, Dad and Mother had had an argument. Mom felt I would put Dad in a better mood before coming in for the meal. Sometimes he would come to supper right away, and other times it took him awhile. When Dad wouldn't come in right away, I would make small talk, and Dad just listened. Finally I would say, "I'm really getting hungry." Dad would sigh, smile, and swing the hoe over his shoulder. Taking me by the hand, we would return to the house. It was clear they had their disagreements, but I never remember Mother and Dad ever arguing in front of their children.

One of the new vegetables Mother grew in the garden was mustard and turnip greens. She would send me to the garden to cut the huge green leaves for dinner. I loved that job, but I couldn't quite figure out something. I could bring in a big armful of greens, and yet when Mother served them for supper there was just a nice-sized bowl full of them.

As the pre-teen and teenage years approached the older children, it ushered in a new set of challenges for Mother and Dad. None of us were angels, and everyone had their faults. Some had a bad habit of talking back to Mother, and Mom was not beyond physical punishment. Her theory was "spare the rod, spoil the child." For these occasions she would go outside to cut a willow stick for spanking.

Mary always ran away from Mother if she knew she was going to get spanked. If Mother was especially upset after trying to catch Mary, she would spank any child in sight. The rest of the children that were outside ran for cover. I was small and often indoors watching my little brother Jerry. Mother would finally come in the house. In the midst of Mother's anger, I often got the brunt of it. I would never run away from Mom as I hadn't caused her to be angry. Still, I experienced her whippings as she vented. I would protest through tears, saying, "I didn't do anything!" Mother would respond by explaining the punishment would apply toward all the times I should have gotten hit but didn't. One time Mom hit me especially hard with the whip. It cut the back of my leg open. It took a long time to heal because the cut was so deep. To this day I still have the scar.

Mother and Dad must have worked out arrangements as to who was going to discipline the children. It seemed to me that Dad took over correcting the boys and Mother was left to correct the girls. Their discipline was more successful on some than others. Sometimes it seemed that they just had to put up with the misbehavior, as it really didn't change over the years. Mary became a tomboy and stayed out of Mother's fury as much as possible. I was happy when Mother stopped using the willow branch. The next time you see a willow tree, notice how thin the branches are. The branch acts as a whip. It would often wrap around your leg and provided long red marks/welts. Mother always aimed for the legs, but sometimes she would miss and hit elsewhere.

I was very upset with Mother during these times. I was equally upset with Mary as she was often responsible for getting Mom in such a bad mood. Mary and I would often argue over these issues. As I grew older I began to speak my mind more openly with my brothers and sisters. Sometimes I was even able to tell Mom when I thought she was being unfair. These were not arguments, just discussion. Mother always defended her position and told me that there were always "two sides to every story."

Sometimes I just needed time alone. On these occasions I would walk the farm's fields. There was a big, tall tree near the back of the property where I took refuge. I could be found there often over the next several years. Sometimes it was after spankings, but as the years passed it was more for solitude and peace of mind. One day I was in a melancholy mood. It was a misty, rainy kind of day. I needed to go for a walk. I went to my tree to daydream about a better life when I grew up. I thought all the things young children think about. I was gone quite a while, and when I returned in the rain, I was afraid Mom would scold me. Instead Mother asked, "Where have you been?" I told her I went for a walk back by the big tree. Mom gazed thoughtfully at me like she understood completely. She told me in a quiet voice to change my clothes before I "catch my death of cold." This was another one of Mother's sayings.

Of course there were happy moments as well. One winter Dad took Mary and I to the schoolyard where there was an ice pond. Dad was going to teach us how to skate. We spent more time falling down than standing, and there was a lot of laughter that day. This was my only experience ice skating with my dad. While I never learned how to skate, there was great joy in trying to learn.

Then there were free movie nights in the summertime! These were hosted by a village a few miles down the road. Dad loaded us in the car, but he could never seem to get Mother to come along. She said she had too much work to do and that Jerry was too little to go. We were always disappointed to leave without her. On reflection, I think Mom really used those evenings for some much-needed peace and quiet.

The older children often enjoyed movie going on Sunday afternoons. I wanted to go too, but they never wanted me to go with them. They felt I was too much trouble and they didn't want to baby-sit. Mother and Dad made them take me though, or they couldn't go at all. The movies opened up a whole new world for me. I loved musicals the best. Everyone had pretty clothes, went to parities, and danced! There were beautiful houses, fancy cars, and lots of money to spend. What a life! It was fuel for my daydreams when I went back to my tree.

Mother and Dad were kind and loving people. They loved us very much and made many sacrifices for us. They worked hard to provide the necessities of life. They did not yell. There were never arguments in front of us. Dad was the type of guy who would go for long walks to cool off rather than argue. I never saw Dad angry or unkind. It just wasn't in him. Mother felt she needed to be the disciplinarian of the family. She may not have gotten it right all the time, but she too had a good heart. Mother preferred to scold than yell, and that was accompanied by a stern look. On occasion (in desperation), she resorted to other more "physical" measures.

Mom was tired, overworked, and concerned for the future of her children. She taught us the "Golden Rule" (do unto others as you would have them do unto you), and believed in it firmly. Other favorite moral expressions and clichés included:

*"People who live in glass houses shouldn't throw stones."*
*"Don't judge others until you walk in their shoes."*
*"The grass is always greener on the other side of the fence."*

These were just a few; there were so many more.

Some of the neighborhood boys would meet at the schoolhouse and hang out. Often Roland and Andrew would join them. One evening someone decided to kick in a panel of the school door. Later it was reported to the police. The culprit tried to lay the blame on Roland. While Roland denied the accusation, he would not identify the boy who really did it. The police finally solved the mystery by matching boot prints on the door, and discovered the identity of the vandal. While Roland was proved innocent, Mother and Dad insisted upon paying for part of the repair. They wanted to instill in Roland a sense of responsibility and the need to honor the family's good name.

Mother believed in Catholic education, and Roland and Catherine continued to go to the Catholic high school. After my third-grade experience, I went back to the one-room schoolhouse with Andy and Mary.

Roland and Jerry were Mother's favorites. Andy didn't seem to get the attention the other boys did. As a little boy, Andy was very shy and quiet. He hated school and learning was a real struggle for him. Growing up, he socialized with Roland's friends. These boys were older. Roland and his friends would use "colorful" language and soon started smoking. Roland's friends picked on Andy because he was younger. They called him a "softy." Dad and Roland told Andy he would have to learn how to deal with these boys or ignore them. It was difficult for Andy to ignore them, and he chose a different path. He became very tough. He learned how to yell, swear, smoke, and fight. He lost a good many battles in the beginning, but eventually he got good at it. Because he hated school, he wanted to quit when he was in the eighth grade. Mother and Dad argued for hours with him, but in the end they let him quit. Andy learned how to drive and did lots of odd jobs. I never saw Andy as a tough guy; he just seemed to be a nice brother. We never fought and got along well together.

The world loomed large beyond our lives and family. By the late thirties and early forties, vast changes were occurring on the political and economic fronts. The Depression was ending, and President Roosevelt was successful in getting America moving forward again. On the European front, however, the winds of war were blowing. In 1939 the Nazi movement led by Adolf Hitler caused great concern. Poland, Denmark, and Norway soon fell to this ambitious leader's drive for power. France would soon succumb as well, and everyone knew that England would be next on Hitler's agenda. America began strengthening itself both economically and militarily, but in the midst of its growth and productivity, the country fell under attack. Italy and Japan allied themselves with Hitler's attempt to rule the world. Japan bombed Pearl Harbor on December 7, 1941, and America was immersed in World War II. This terrible war would eventually cause great death and destruction. It caused serious hardship on both soldier and citizen between 1941 and 1945, and only the invention and implementation of the atomic bomb against Japan would cause it to end the war.

During this era there were huge changes in the American workplace. The auto factories were re-tooled to manufacture war machinery. The young men were drafted, leaving a shortage of workers. Women began to take jobs in the factories to fill the need. The work movement for women initiated in this period would begin a transformation that continues even today.

Dad transferred to the tank arsenal and worked long hours. He made very good money working fifty to sixty hours a week. He felt proud to do his part to help America win the war. He had an opportunity to go to night school to learn the tool and die trade. Because Dad had a great personality, he was respected by the men and was soon promoted to a foreman's position. Despite his good fortune, Dad would often remark that he would rather see the boys home from the war, even if it meant he had to stand in a bread line for food. He was not pleased that men were dying while he was making good money. He often referred to the income as "blood money."

Mother and Dad considered education the key to getting ahead in life. Their children didn't seem to catch the vision. Roland and Catherine dropped out of school before graduating. Motivated by a desire to buy cars and clothes, the lure of money was very strong. Mother and Dad were very disappointed. They sincerely wished they would have graduated from high school before getting a job.

Roland and Catherine found employment in a supermarket. Roland's future looked bright, and he had his eyes set on an assistant manager's position. However, the military had other ideas. To avoid being drafted in the Army, Roland chose to enlist in the Navy. This devastated Mom. She couldn't stand the thought of his leaving, not knowing if he would ever return.

In order to cope with the emotional devastation from Roland's enlistment, Mother took a job at a local hospital caring for the elderly. She became one of the cooks. Mom was deeply impacted by the number of elderly people who seemed abandoned by their families and left alone to die. She came home many nights in tears, vowing that she never wanted to be placed in a nursing home. Despite the emotional weight of taking care of the elderly, she found comfort in cooking for them, and it did alleviate some of the pain she suffered over Roland's leaving.

Mother began making care-mail packages to send to Roland. She learned to make delicious candies and other goodies for him. That provoked some jealousy in the rest of the children, as they were not the recipients. Mother wouldn't make extras because there was a ration on some food products, particularly sugar. Mom made just enough to send to Roland. Mother tried to explain to us that Roland was making a large sacrifice in the service of his country. As brothers and sisters, we should be willing to make the much smaller sacrifice of forgoing candy treats! She reminded us that it was men like Roland who were keeping the country safe, and we shouldn't complain.

Dad's oldest son Paul (from Maine), was also in the Navy. Mother and Dad would write his other children over the years. Paul knew where Dad lived and came to see him when he was stationed at the Great Lakes Naval Base. It was wonderful meeting him. He looked just like Dad (only Dad was better looking). When it came to the ladies and the stories his son would tell, Dad knew the "apple didn't fall far from the tree." His daughters Pauline and Christine both married brothers. Their husbands were also in the service. Dad's son from his first marriage was named Everett. He had joined the Marines and was killed overseas in the battle of Iwo Jima. Dad's daughter Dorothy felt very alone after her brother died, and she longed to reestablish ties with her father sometime in the future.

Dad felt the pain of having his children serve during the war. He recognized the need to turn his life over to God. He wanted to pray for his children, especially for their protection and safe return home from war. He decided it was time to become Catholic. Mother was thrilled with Dad's decision, as were we all. This was a special time for Dad and Mother, as they were now united in faith.

About the time I was ready for sixth grade, Mom wanted me to return to St. Mary's Catholic school. I rode to school with several older neighbor children down the road. They were not considered as poor as our family, and once again I took a lot of teasing because of my worn out hand-me-down clothes. This made for very unpleasant trips to school.

On Saturdays I would go with Mother and Dad to the 5 & 10 cent store. I met a girl I knew from school. We stopped to talk. After a few minutes, Mom came up to me and told me they were ready to leave. I would meet them in the car. As Mom walked away, the girl asked if she was my mother. I responded yes, and this young girl went on to talk about how beautiful Mother was. That struck me, as I had never considered my mother to be beautiful in quite that context. Mom never wore any makeup and her hair was kept long (rolled up in a bun in the back). She wore old barn shoes most of the time, and her coat had holes that were pinned closed to keep out the cold in the winter. Her dresses were faded, purchased years ago at the dime store. Was Mom beautiful? What did she see that I was missing? Beautiful women wore makeup. They had nice clothes, fancy shoes, and smelled pretty. This was my concept of beauty. At that age, I guess it is sometimes hard to see the forest through the trees.

The chime of the old mantle clock had stopped working, and Dad missed that. They decided to have it fixed. After the repair, Dad loved having the clock back home again. He took the responsibility of winding it regularly. He was so proud of that mantle clock! He was still waiting for his ship to come in. When that happened, they would have so many beautiful things. The clock would remain in a place of honor. Mother told Dad he gave that clock way too much attention. She felt they already had plenty of things to be thankful for. She reminded him to count the blessings he already had! The mantle clock never stayed working for long, and Mother said no more money would be spent on fixing it again. Dad kept in on the mantle anyway.

When I was twelve years old, I took a job caring for a neighbor's four children. It was an ambitious summer job that was supposed to go to my older sister Mary. The neighbor children never took a liking to Mary, so Mother and Dad suggested that I give it a try. The parents were leery of the idea because I seemed young for such a large responsibility. Plus, their oldest was a girl just one year younger than I was!

They decided to give me a chance. I got up every day at 5:00 a.m. My day consisted of cleaning the house and preparing all meals (including starting the dinner meal to make things easier on the mother when she returned from her work). I got back home around 5:30 p.m. I got along fine all summer, but there were nights when I was especially tired. On occasion I was told that I would walk in my sleep. I would sleepwalk to the kitchen and start preparing food to cook. Mother would try to wake me and send me back to bed. Mom felt the job was too much for me, but she let me finish out the summer. I have no memory of my sleepwalking days! I was paid $20.00 a week for my twelve-hour-a-day job. I gave my income to Mother and the money helped with our family expenses.

One fall, Mom bought Mary and I two new winter coats. It was the first time Mother was able to buy two new coats in the same season. Unfortunately, neither Mary nor I liked the coats (Mary's was purple and mine was light beige). Mary was quite vocal and told Mom how she felt. Mother's feelings were hurt, and I felt bad that Mary had spoken up. While I didn't particularly like my coat, I was thrilled to have a new one instead of a hand-me-down.

On one occasion Mom asked me to stay with a neighbor woman who was ill. I didn't want to go. I would have to give up my entire afternoon! Mother laid a guilt trip on me and recited the corporal works of mercy (part of our religious faith). A specific work includes visiting the sick. I walked over to the neighbor, wondering how Mom remembered all those "works" and could recite them so quickly. Who taught her all that stuff anyway? When I returned home later that day, Mother asked me how it went. I told her it turned out to be a great afternoon! She was the funniest lady I had ever met. Mother was pleased.

Now that I was getting a little older, I noticed that after dinner Mom would sit at the table and drink her tea. This was a sort of ritual that she would enjoy before going out to help Dad and the boys with the evening

Mother and Dad
The summer of 1940

chores. I wanted to have some tea too! Mother told me that I was too young to drink tea. Still, I was able to sit with Mom, and we would talk for a while. During these conversations I would ask Mother questions about what it was like for her when she was growing up. Mom would tell me stories from her childhood in Ireland. As time went on, our talks became more frequent.

Mother never wanted us to consider ourselves poor. She felt we were rich in blessings and had so many things to be thankful for. As I grew older I found it difficult to be that thankful all the time. Wearing old clothes bothered me, and I was envious of those who had indoor bathrooms and hot running water for baths or showers. It seemed that life was filled with nothing but dawn-to-dusk work. I really wanted more out of life than that. Mother and Dad worked so very hard and never seemed to get enough help for all that needed doing.

One day Dad brought Mother a beautiful gift. Inside a large, velvet, wine-colored box was a twenty-four karat gold-plated set of jewelry. It included a necklace with earrings and a bracelet. There were many pink stones set in the bands of gold. Mother really loved the set but was upset with Dad for spending the money. She hardly ever wore the jewelry but kept it in a special place in their bedroom (along with her beautiful watch). This was not jewelry you'd wear to the corner grocery store, and Mom rarely went much farther than that!

Around Christmastime, Mother would put an ad in

the newspaper in order to sell fresh turkeys. She got quite a response. The night before deliveries she would work late into the night plucking feathers. No one wanted any part of that kind of work! I didn't want to do that work either, but Mom needed some help. I would stay up with her despite the fact that Mother kept telling me to go to bed and get some sleep. Finally, late in the night, I would go upstairs to bed, trying not to wake my sleeping sisters. I would lie sideways at the foot of the bed so as not to disturb them. I was so tired I didn't even take the time to take off my clothes. In the morning the girls would run down and tell Mom that I had slept in my clothes. Mother knew the story and told them to leave me alone and let me sleep.

Roland would usually deliver the turkeys to the families in the Mt. Clemens area. The year that he was in service, Mother asked Andy and I to do it. Andy (who loved to drive), was good to go. I was more apprehensive but off we went. Andy was in charge of finding the house, and I was to take the turkey up to the door. On one stop I walked up to a door and rang the doorbell. A big, tall, black man answered. I looked at him, and he looked at me and asked, "Little girl, what can I do for you?" I held up the turkey and said, "Here's your turkey!" The man roared with laughter and said, "Little girl, I think you have the wrong house." I ran back to the car very shaken. I was upset with Andy for taking me to the wrong house.

Andy, Mother, and Dad would laugh about that story for some time.

One of the new foods that came on the market at that time was margarine. It came in a one-pound package and looked like lard. It was white in color, but they gave you a little yellow liquid pill. You mixed this pill in the white lard to make it turn yellow. The result was yellow-colored margarine. Did it taste like butter? No, but Mother said we weren't going to make homemade butter anymore. I did love to mix the new margarine and watch as it turned from white to yellow. It was so easy! It took me a few weeks to get good at it, but making homemade butter was one less chore Mother now had to do.

During our years on the farm, Mother's brother Mike would visit from time to time. When he first came over from Ireland, he was working on a farm. He then married and bought his own farm. He couldn't make a go of it and lost it. Then they moved to Detroit where he got a job with the Grand Trunk Railroad. For several reasons, Uncle Mike started drinking. He would stop at the bars daily on his way home. Things got really bad for him; he often became quite drunk.

Somehow he would make his way to our house. Often he would stumble in during the middle of the night and would stay for several days. Mother would sober him up and tried hard to put him back on the right track. I would often hear him sobbing as he talked about how unhappy he was. He hated his job on the railroad and loved farming. He was unhappy in his marriage but felt trapped and didn't know what to do. The conversations went on for hours. Mother told him repeatedly that drinking was not an answer. He would always return home, but several months later he would be back again. He always turned to his older sister for compassion. Mother told us that Uncle Mike was too fond of the "bottle." Mom prayed that her boys would never turn to drinking. She hated the bottle!

Catherine had left school and was now working. She enjoyed buying nice clothes and wearing makeup. She looked very pretty. Mary wanted to do the same thing, so she soon quit school as well. Mother and Dad were very disappointed. They had only two children left and hoped they would finish high school.

Now that I was getting older, Mary and I occasionally went to the movies with some of the neighborhood boys on Sunday afternoon. We were never allowed to go in the evening (we were too young for that), and these were never "dates." The boys were simply neighborhood friends. One time we went out to eat after the show. We got home later than usual. Mother greeted the boys with a baseball bat! She was very upset. The boys explained frantically that everyone had gone out for a snack. Eventually Mom calmed down. While it didn't seem funny at the time, Mom and I would share a lot of laughs over the years recalling that episode. Like all parents,

Mother and Dad found raising children through the teen years both challenging and difficult.

I also remember the winter when Mary and I were allowed to go tobogganing with some of the neighbor boys. They were all between twelve and fourteen years old, but some of the boys that age were allowed to drive—and even had their own used cars!

One boy who had a car decided to hook a toboggan to the back of his vehicle. He wanted to pull us down the dirt road. I was wearing an old hand-me-down coat. There wasn't enough snow to slide on, as the road was gravel. I started to feel the bottom of my coat getting warm. We yelled at the boys to stop the car, and finally they did. A hole had burned through the bottom of the toboggan, and another hole was starting to burn through my winter coat. Needless to say, when Mother heard what happened we were scolded for doing such a foolish thing. Life's lessons are best learned the first time around. One needs to know the difference between danger and fun. These were valuable life lessons that Mother and Dad always tried to teach.

I began taking an interest in learning to play piano. Dad and Mother bought a used one, and I began taking lessons from the mayor's wife in Mt. Clemens. To pay for the cost of the lessons, I cleaned the woman's house before my lesson. I loved her house and thought she had many beautiful things in it. A very big, beautiful Tiffany lamp was a valued item that I was never allowed to touch.

Mother and Dad were proud that I was learning to play the piano. Dad loved to sit and listen to me practice. His favorite song was, "I'll Take You Home Again, Kathleen." It reminded him of Mother. My siblings were a bit jealous of the piano and my newly acquired skill. They complained, but Mom and Dad brushed aside their complaints. A few years prior, they had given Roland the opportunity to play the trumpet. There were complaints about that too. Dad and Mother would have given anyone of their children similar opportunities had anyone else shown an interest. I took lessons for two years. I realized I would never be a great pianist. I also knew it was a sacrifice for Mom and Dad. It was a long drive each week to and from the mayor's house. While inconvenient, Dad would drive me. I think it was a labor of love.

Catherine was the first to marry. She married a neighbor boy named Clarence who lived across the road. Mary and I stood up in the wedding as attendants. It seemed like such a wonderful wedding. I got all dressed up in a blue gown with a big blue bonnet to match. Mary's dress was the same style, only in pink. This was my first experience at a formal affair, and I really enjoyed being dressed up. The music and dancing were also wonderful. I loved listening to the band late into the evening. It probably wasn't the grandest wedding in the world, but at the impressionable age of thirteen, it was the nicest social event I had ever attended. Mother had concerns about Catherine's marriage, fearful of her new husband's drinking habits. What would the future hold for them?

Dad's hours at the factory were cut back when the war ended. Mother continued working in order to supplement the family income. We were buying more food at the store now and raising less. The local store let us charge food one month at a time. Every month Mother and Dad would take their paychecks and pay off the grocery charges. This was a frequent practice for stores who serviced large families. Sometimes the food bill exceeded our means. Mother felt that paying bills was a real balancing act. She often said that she had to "rob Peter to pay Paul."

Despite the difficulty of these years, Mom never complained. Dad continued to joke about when his ship would come in. Everyone went along with the jest, while Mother kept reminding him to count his blessings.

Mother soon learned about dairy farming and wanted to give it a try. Gardening was getting to be too much work. Again, Dad was not thrilled but went along with the idea. Dad always said Mom was the boss. Mother believed that dairy cows would help bring in a bigger income. I heard that there might be an upcoming move and was ecstatic. I hoped I had plucked my last turkey!

# Chapter VII

The farm was about a half-mile away from where we had been living on Fairchild Road. It was quite large, about sixty acres. A portion of it was rather hilly. Early in the farm's history (before a fire destroyed most of the large home), it was considered to be the most modern farm in the area. When I first saw it, I thought the farmland was beautiful. From the front the land facing the road was full of small, rolling hills. There was a long, curved driveway that went up a hill to get to the house. I envisioned what the farmhouse would have looked liked before being destroyed. It had been the envy of all the neighbors.

After the original owners died, it was left to their only daughter. She sold it to Mother and Dad. Mom saw the hills as a goldmine. They were sand hills, not good for farming. Mother and Dad sold the sand to a trucking company. While it brought in money, the farm never looked the same after the hills were removed. Much of the farm's natural beauty was gone.

With the money they got from the sand, they were able to jumpstart the dairy farming operation. The farm had a large barn that was in good condition. They bought more cows and a better tractor. They bought electric milking machines and a cooler for the milk house. The milk house even had hot water! They sold the milk to a local creamery company for added income.

What was left of the partially destroyed house was a living room, a small kitchen area (with one small hand sink with faucets that had running water), and two small rooms used for bedrooms. Mary and I got one of the bedrooms. It was very small and just big enough for a bed. The floor of the bedroom was below the level of the rest of the house. This made the room very damp and gloomy. I hated the bedroom and made my feelings known. Mom told me to make the best of it. Dad soon added on another bedroom and a living room. The previous living room became a dining room. Everyone felt we had come up in the world! We still had an outside toilet, however.

After the war, the tank arsenal closed down. Dad left Hudson Motor Car. There just wasn't enough work. He found a new job and went to work at Mt. Clemens General Hospital. With his great personality, he was soon respected by the physicians that ran the hospital. He was offered a supervisory position in the laundry, along with other duties in maintenance and boiler operations. With the promotion came a raise in pay. I remember overhearing Dad telling Mom how much money he was going to be making (a hundred dollars a week)! They both seemed to be so excited and happy. When I walked in, they knew I had heard their discussion. Mother wanted me to promise that I wouldn't tell anyone (for fear that people would think they were rich). However, I was very happy. One hundred dollars a week! We were all thrilled.

To celebrate this happy occasion, Dad bought a television. As he never had any money of his own, he charged it. He was so happy when he brought it home. He didn't tell anyone he was doing this because he wanted to surprise the family. Mother was furious when she found out. She didn't speak to him for days. She felt it was a total waste of money. This was a luxury they couldn't afford and didn't need. What was wrong with just listening to the radio?

When the family would gather around to watch television in the evening, Mother refused to come into the room. It took a while for her to come around, but within a few weeks she started watching the news. Before long she was watching all the programs with the rest of us.

Soon after Dad got his job, Mother went to work for him in the laundry. Her job was to iron (by hand) all of the doctor's white uniforms. She worked in a very small room that got very hot. When I would visit her each day after high school, I asked how she could work in all that heat. Mother responded, "Hard work never hurt anybody," a phrase I had heard so many times before. I would spend the rest of my time with Mother doing homework and waiting to go home with Mom and Dad at the end of the day.

The hours they worked at the hospital were just a portion of their day. In the morning and evening they would have to do all the farm chores (feeding and milking the cows, etc). They continued to grow vegetable crops and labored long hours during the spring and summer seasons. Mother and Dad soon found out the days were endless. Mom would often repeat "there just aren't enough hours in a day."

Mother went to the "old folks' home" to get a man to help them out with the chores. His name was Steve. He was happy to come and work for room and board, as he hated living in the senior home. We provided him with an old shed to live in. He would come inside our house for his meals. One of his favorite foods for dinner was limburger cheese. It smelled up the whole house and everyone complained. Mother felt he was entitled to have his cheese every once in a while. Dad was uneasy with Steve being around us. Mother assured Dad that Steve was harmless. He stayed on the farm for some time until his health failed, and Mom had to send him back to the home.

Steve had a very unusual hobby. He carried with him little bits of paper he had collected. These papers were always with him. After dinner he would take out his pipe for a smoke and then arrange his papers in several different ways on the dining room table. He would do this for an hour or more before going back to his little shed for the night. I would ask Mom why he did this. She explained that those papers were all that he had left in the world. They were his treasures. I felt so sad for him. To realize all he had left in life were small bits of paper. I shared my feelings with Mom. She told me many of the people at the "home" had nothing at all to live for, not even bits of papers! This is why Mother told us over and over again that she never wanted to be placed in an old folks' home when she got old.

All the farmers would help each other out during harvest time. It was expected that the women would provide the main meal for all. It was to be a hearty meal, as the men worked very hard. Other farmers considered Mother and Dad to be "small-time" farmers. It would only take a small crew to help them during the harvesting. I was asked by different farm women to help with the cooking and cleaning during harvest season. They had big beautiful farm homes with large dining rooms and kitchens. I felt ashamed to have their men come over to our humble home. Our house had so few conveniences in comparison. We were considered to be "poor" farmers by some. Mother chided me for feeling this way. She reminded me that we were blessed and should be thankful for what we did have. After cooking and baking for hours, it was sometimes challenging to remain ever so thankful.

After the harvest meal, the men would sit around and smoke. The old timers would often tell stories about the "good old days." One such story described how Whiskey Road got its name. We were told that during Prohibition, whiskey was smuggled in hay wagons down the road from the railroad tracks. Back then it was a narrow, muddy, dirt road. I would smile as I envisioned these hay wagons going up and down the road full of whiskey. After all, the road was gravel surfaced now and was wide enough for two cars to pass! Years later the county renamed all the local roads, and Whiskey Road became 23 Mile Road.

On his weekends, Dad would get the fields ready for planting during spring and fall. This was the only extra time he had. On one hot spring day, Mom made Dad a lunch. She asked me to take his lunch out to him in the fields. I took the long walk back to where he was plowing with the tractor. He stopped the tractor under a tree as he saw me coming. I wanted to be of help while he was eating, and I said I would drive the tractor while he ate and rested. This was fine with Dad. I had never driven a tractor before, and he gave me some very brief instructions. Off I went driving up and down the field. After time had passed, I realized Dad had gone to sleep under the tree. Every time I passed by the tree I would call out to him. He was so tired that he never heard me. He had also forgotten to show me how to stop the tractor! After about a half hour or so, Dad finally woke up. He caught up to me and stopped the tractor. I thought I'd be on that tractor forever!

I was a little shaken, but Dad told me he was sorry. He smiled all through the apology though. I walked back to the house and told Mom what happened. She had wondered what took me so long but was laughing though our entire conversation. Dad and Mother teased me about that incident for some time to come.

I soon got to be too big to sit on my dad's knee anymore. It was awkward for us both to no longer have that father/daughter connection in quite the same way. Dad started to hold my hand as an alternative. This was an expression we could use to help sustain the closeness between us. I would also enjoy sitting next to him in the evening when we watched television.

Uncle Mike heard about our move to the new farm. When he came to visit us, he was still in his usual condition. Uncle Mike never lost his strong Irish accent. He continued his tradition of singing Irish songs on the evening of the first night that he would stay over. I enjoyed hearing him sing, but along with the rest of the family—we needed sleep!

One day Mother got a call from her sister-in-law, Mary. Her husband, Mike, had been drinking. While walking home from the bar he was struck by a hit and run driver. Uncle Mike was in the hospital and his injuries were serious. He would remain in the hospital for some time. One Sunday, Mother and Dad went to see him.

The hospital was a long distance from where we were living, and they were gone most of the day.

When they returned home, Mother was very sad. Mom and I talked for a long time. I listened as she told me about their day. Her brother no longer recognized her. In fact, he didn't recognize anyone. This hurt her deeply. She talked to the doctors about his condition and possible recovery. She was told that between his accident injuries and his chronic alcoholism, it was unlikely that he would ever regain his memory.

A short time after we had that talk, Uncle Mike died. I remember how this impacted Mother and understood her sorrow and her growing hatred for alcohol (which contributed to Mike's death). My brothers Roland and Andrew were now young men. They were at that age when drinking was a popular thing to do. Dad had always set a good example for his children (he rarely ever had a drink), but it would be difficult for Mother and Dad to discourage their sons from the lure of alcohol.

Mother and Dad's favorite drink was tea. When I was growing up I always wanted to drink tea. As a teenager it was now permitted. Mom and I would often be the last ones at the table, and we would talk while drinking our tea. On Sunday afternoons, Mother didn't have to go out to the barns. These were times for conversation as well, and we would talk for hours. Mom would tell me stories about her life on the farm in Ireland. I loved to listen to Mom's stories. These were special times for us even though I didn't fully appreciate that back then. They were the beginning of a special tradition we would maintain through the years. Mom and I cherished our "tea times."

One day I noticed that the mantle clock was gone! Evidently it never made the move to our dairy farm. Did Mother and Dad discuss throwing the clock away? Did it just disappear? I missed the clock and all that it meant to Dad. I hoped that one day he would get another one. That never happened.

One weekend my girlfriend from across the road wanted to go square dancing with her uncle. She wanted me to go along with them. It was a long distance to the dance hall, and Mother wasn't keen on letting me go. After much pleading, I was given permission.

I fell in love with dancing! Even though all the people at the dance were older than we were, they treated us as their daughters. I learned to do all kinds of different dances (square dancing, waltzes, polkas, etc.). I wanted to go every weekend! When I shared my love of dancing with Mom, the stories reminded her of her younger days in Ireland with her father. Still, she was very reluctant to let me go because she felt the dance hall was too far away.

On one Saturday night, Roland showed up at the hall. We tried to get him involved in the fun, but Roland wanted no part of it. He sat in a chair until it was time to take us home. I later realized that Mother sent Roland to "check out the place" and to make sure it was okay for us to be there.

Soon after, a new dance hall opened in the neighborhood closer to our home. All the local young people would go there. It was a great place to dance, and Mother felt much better about letting me attend. She knew I loved to dance because that was all I would talk about! I lived for the weekends. On one particular Friday night, Andy showed up at the hall. This was very odd, as Andy was usually out drinking with his friends. He was not fond of dances or social affairs, and he had a reputation as a guy you wouldn't want to mess around with. He could cuss and fight (if need be) and wasn't afraid to take on anybody who crossed his path. All the local boys knew that and paid heed. Andy kept his distance while at the dance and stayed at the other side of the hall so he wouldn't interfere with me and my friends.

As fate would have it, some "city boys" from town stopped by that very same night. One boy came up to me and asked me to do the jitterbug. This was a new dance that we all enjoyed. Part of the dance included a flip (the boy would flip the girl over his shoulder, down his back, and the girl was to land on her feet). Flips were usually reserved for professional dancers in the movies. I didn't want any part of flipping! We wore dresses or skirts in those days, and slacks were not an option for a dance. I was considered a good dancer but mainly danced with the local boys who danced well too. The local boys knew I didn't like flipping and respected my wishes.

I told the city boy I would dance with him but there would be no flip. He agreed from the start, but as we were dancing, he tried to get cute and flip me anyway. I fought the flip all the way to the floor and landed on my bottom. I was very embarrassed. The boy and his friends were laughing. Andy had witnessed the entire episode, and it was more than he could handle. He flew off his seat, grabbed the boy, had him on the floor, and within seconds really punched him out. I tried to explain to Andy that I was okay, but it took some shouting to get through. A few local boys helped me pull Andy off the city boy and let him go. The boy and his friends made one quick mad dash for the door!

I doubt Andy was there to check up on me, but I do think he may have been curious as to why I liked going there all the time. Mother always waited up for me to come home, and when she asked me how the dance went I told her what happened. Mother was furious with Andy. Fighting was not acceptable behavior, and she felt the family's good name could be tarnished by brawling. I didn't see it that way and was very proud of my brother for defending my honor. Andy has always held a special place in my heart.

Around this time, Dad had a heart attack. I couldn't see him for a several days as his condition was critical. Mom and the older children were the only ones allowed at the hospital. When I was finally able to visit him in the hospital room, I saw him with tubes in his arms and heart machines by his side. It was time for Dad to have a meal, and he couldn't even feed himself. This upset me a great deal, as I loved my dad dearly. I remembered all the good times we had. I prayed that he would be okay and come home soon.

Tea time took on new topics that I felt I needed to express my opinions on. I was considered to be the most outspoken member of all the siblings. I knew Mother and Dad worked hard from morning till night. I knew how some in the family didn't always carry their share of the workload. I knew how some of my siblings borrowed money that Mother and Dad really didn't have to give. Over the years I shared my opinion on these situations and felt that Mom was generous to a fault. Mother needed to save money for their future and not give it away! How would they ever have anything when they retired? Dad would often overhear these conversations and agreed with me. He usually said very little though, so as not to cause hurt feelings between the two of them. I considered the problem to be of serious concern, and it was a point that Mother and I often disagreed on. She believed that in giving you receive, while I suspected that they might be taken advantage of.

Roland was the next to marry. He met and married a girl named Bertha. It was a big wedding, and I was one of the bridesmaids. This was my second time as a bridesmaid, and I loved getting all dressed up. I now knew how to dance well and had a great time.

Roland and Bertha built a house on Fairchild Road. Catherine and Clarence had built a house on 23 Mile Road. Dad helped out with the construction of both homes. They were small, simple homes, and nothing lavish. The family was very proud of their homes. Mother and Dad felt that their children were getting a good start in life.

Mary began dating a man named Bob and married very quickly. Mother and Dad provided them with a small, simple wedding. Mary and Bob bought a small house on Fairchild Road, not far from the farm. Mother and Dad loved having their children living nearby.

Andy, Jerry, and I were the only children now at home. I became close to both of my brothers. I spent many hours every day taking care of Jerry. Mom was working, so he became my responsibility during the day. We both got along well, as we were the youngest in the family.

Andy hoped to open a welding shop and have his own business. Mother and Dad loaned him the money to get started. The shop lasted only a few months. It was a bad investment for everyone. Andy was very disappointed. Dad felt bad for Andy because he knew success would have meant a lot to him.

I was still in high school, working part time after school at the 5 & 10 cent store. I was making $7.42 a week. I took the bus home every night and sometimes had money left over to buy a few things. I relished the opportunity to get *new* clothes and *new* shoes! Mother worried I was becoming materialistic. She would say, "It's not what you put on your back that counts, but what's inside."

One summer I went to work full time at the local grocery store. This was the same store that I had taken the apple from as a young girl. Dad was pleased that the owner didn't hold a grudge, as my parents took pride in the family name. They always paid their bills, never took handouts, and got along on what they had. Mother and Dad kept a running tab on their groceries. Now that I was working there I found out many families did the same. I began to realize that there were many people in the community that were struggling. Sometimes it seemed Dad and Mother actually had more than others! If the end of the month arrived before the entire bill was paid, the store owner would carry over the balance due to the next month. The owner loved the first of the month when the families were to pay their accounts. I found out that more often than not, the adding machine would break down during these times. I had to add up all the meat and groceries by hand on a big brown paper bag. I disliked it at the time, but I got really fast at adding numbers!

I continued attending the weekend dances. I had the company of girlfriends and some of the local neighborhood boys. I didn't have a boyfriend yet. On one Friday night a group of guys from the "big city" (Mt. Clemens), came out to the hall to check out the girls. One was called Joe. He took a liking to one of my girlfriends. Joe and his buddies started to come to the dances on a regular basis. They were well liked by all the locals. After the dance, the guys would go out for a bite to eat. Joe invited my girlfriend, but her mother wouldn't let her go (she felt she was too young to go out). In time, Joe and I became good friends. He started asking me to dance, and we made very good dance partners. Joe started asking me out for a bite to eat after the dance. I went with him as a friend. I learned that Joe had been in the military service, had been sent overseas, and had "seen the world."

In my eyes it seemed he had done well for himself. Could this be the man of my dreams? Over time the relationship became serious, and the rest is history!

Mom really liked Joe. She felt I had found a "good catch." During our courtship Joe and I had an argument and broke up. We decided to give back the gifts we both exchanged over Christmas (returning gifts after a break up was the customary thing to do during those years). A week went by, and I never heard from Joe. I questioned Mom about this. Mother suggested I call him. I didn't want to do that because back then it wasn't considered "proper" for a girl to call a guy. Mom finally convinced me to call him. Joe was very friendly, and during the conversation we set up a date and started seeing each other again. A few weeks went by and Joe asked why I never returned his gifts, as he had returned mine. Mother never told me Joe came over one day when I wasn't home! I was upset with Mother as I did not appreciate her trying to be our matchmaker. Still, I wonder. What if Mom had never convinced me to call Joe on the telephone?

Dad liked Joe too. He did feel that I was too young and wasn't fond of the idea of us getting serious. I gave him plenty of time to get used to the idea that his little girl ("the apple of my father's eye") was growing up. Joe and I were married one year later.

Before our marriage, Joe bought an acre of land on a piece of the farm that faced 23 Mile Road. Dad and Mother sold us the property for $140.00 dollars, which is what they had paid per acre. They said they wouldn't make a profit off their own children. Joe, Dad, and Roland built a small home for us to live in after we were married.

During this period of time I quit school in order to get a full-time job. We would need the extra income in order to start our new lives together. Dad and Mother were terribly disappointed. They now had only one child left (Jerry) to fulfill their dream of having one of their children finish high school. I felt bad about this and believed someday I could make this up to them.

Our wedding day was beautiful! Mother and Dad took us and our wedding party out to breakfast at a nice restaurant after Mass. The rest of the day went by quickly. It was a happy occasion. Late that night before I fell asleep I recalled the day's events. I was very grateful for all Mother and Dad had done for us. I was especially grateful for all the work Mom did in preparing the food for the reception. It took her all day to get it ready. She had little to no help but never complained. I felt bad that Mom had to work the entire day of our wedding. I knew that she was exhausted. This was another example of the many sacrifices Mother and Dad made for their children over the years.

Within the first year of our marriage, Joe was called back into military service. He was in the reserves. He was originally drafted into service while in high school, near the end of World War II. It was now the 1950s and the Korean War was starting.

Andy took Joe and me to the bus stop where we said our goodbyes. I was devastated. I had recently found out I was pregnant. We would anticipate the birth of our first child but were concerned for our future. On the way home from the bus stop I managed to keep myself together as best I could. Andy tried to make small talk to try and cheer me up.

We came back to the farm, and I couldn't bring myself to go into the house. I headed for the fields and walked the farm. For days I had this terrible feeling that Joe was never coming back, and that I would never see him again. I brushed these feelings aside while we were together, but now that he was gone these feelings engulfed me. Mother had told me how God always sees me, hears me, and cares for me. She taught me all my prayers when I was just a little girl. In these circumstances though, it just seemed that a few Our Fathers weren't going to cut it.

I entered into a very personal conversation with God. I poured out my heart and soul to Him. Through my tears I begged and pleaded Him to return Joe safely home. I shared with God all of my concerns and all of the dreams for our future. What about a better life for the children? I had quit school to help out, and now I was faced with the prospect of raising a child without an education and a good job. I desperately resisted the idea of being a burden to my parents. After lengthy conversational prayer with God, I began to have a greater sense of peace.

I noticed it was getting dark and there was a chill in the air. It was early fall and the days were getting shorter. With no tears left to cry and my eyes red and swollen, I headed back to the house. I met Dad and Mother as they were leaving to do the evening chores. Dad reached for my hand as I walked in. He joked with me about him and Mom having a date with the cows. I managed a smile while Mom said, "Fix a bite to eat to keep up your strength." Sayings such as these illustrate Dad and Mother's personality. Mom was the practical and down-to-earth mother. Dad was the happy go lucky and loving father.

After four months of marriage, I was home on the farm again with Mom and Dad. Mother knew how I felt about staying in my old bedroom. She told me I could sleep on an old, worn sofa bed in the living room if I wanted. I liked that idea better and felt more peaceful being close to Mother and Dad in the next room. I prayed every night, and afterward I am sure Mother and Dad would hear me crying myself to sleep.

To ease the pain of my loneliness, Andy tried to make my life a little more pleasant. He would ask me out to the movies on many a Friday night. After the movie he would take me out for something to eat. He even took me out for ice cream once in a while. These were special moments as I knew Andy was giving up his own night on the town in order to have ice cream with me. I guess I brought out a different side to Andy. It was a softer side of his personality that he rarely showed to anyone. Most would see this as so unlike Andy, but they were valued times that I recall fondly.

On Saturday mornings Andy would sleep in. When he got up he wanted breakfast. He liked to have a special sausage from a local meat market. However, he didn't like to go to the store to get it, so he asked me to. The meat market was very small. It carried mostly sausage of all kinds. The smoked sausage was hung from the ceiling on long hooks. You could smell the aroma of the different meats. I loved going to that store for Andy. The aroma alone was worth the effort. On returning home I would make him breakfast. This became our weekly ritual. Mother and Dad were happy that Andy and I had such a good relationship. They knew it was good for both of us.

I would write daily letters to Joe. In return I received

several letters each week. One week I didn't receive any letters at all. Soon it was several weeks without any mail. I was terribly concerned. Unknown to me, Mother and Dad went to the Red Cross to see if they could find out if anything happened to Joe. The Red Cross investigated and later contacted Mother and Dad and told them that Joe was wounded in action. They told me what the Red Cross had found out. Joe was in a hospital recovering. Soon he would be sent home to the states.

Two days later I heard the dreaded knock on our door. Military representatives had arrived to make it official. Dad went to the door with me and Mom stood nearby. I saw those young men in full dress uniform, delivering such a serious message. It dawned on me that what I had asked God for was now being granted. While my prayer had been answered, the thought bothered me. I waited until everyone had gone to bed except Mother. We sat down at the dining room table as we had so many others times. Mom knew that something was really bothering me and listened closely.

After Joe had left to go to war, I had prayed that he might be slightly wounded. That way he could come home early but also safely. I realized it may have been an odd prayer, but I was so worried that Joe wasn't coming home for years, or perhaps not at all. If Joe never returned home what would I do? Mom knew my despair as I had struggled with this matter. Dad and Mother had also prayed for Joe and me. Mom and I discussed how tragic it would have been if the military had come for a different reason. We both knew that the knock on the door could have brought a much more serious message. At the end of our talk Mother summed things up, "You'll need to be careful what you pray for." As I look back on these times, one can consider so many "what ifs." I have thanked God daily for His many wonderful blessings.

Joe soon returned to the states. Over the course of time there came one particular Sunday afternoon. He was leaving the house to report back to his base when I went into labor. Mother and Dad took me to the hospital late that evening. It was a long period of labor. I was there all night. Soon I was left alone. I was told the family had all gone home, and that I would have to "make the best of it" by myself. This was a lonesome and difficult experience, but I delivered a beautiful baby girl at about five in the morning. When Mother came to see me, I asked how she arrived so quickly. Mom told me that she was there all night as she didn't want me to be all alone! We were both upset with the nurses for never telling me that she was there the entire night.

The attitude from the nursing staff never seemed to improve. They were very cool and distant. A few days later Joe got special leave from base to come and see me and our new baby. Joe arrived in full dress uniform. He looked very handsome. After he left, one of the nurses became very sheepish. For the first time she spoke kindly, saying, "How nice it was to see your husband." I soon received much better treatment from the nurses after that. Mother and I realized that the nurses thought I was an unwed mother. Unwed mothers were frowned upon in those years. Mom said to me, "People shouldn't be so quick to judge." Within a few weeks, Joe and I went back to our home with the new baby to pick up the pieces of our life.

Mother and Dad were left on the farm with just the two boys, Andy and Jerry. Jerry was now in high school. He was Mother and Dad's last chance to have one of their children graduate. They had high hopes for him. Andy soon met a young woman named Joyce and eventually married. Joyce had been married before and had a little boy. Andy purchased property from Mother and Dad on 23 Mile Road. With some help they built a house to start their life in.

There was a constant flow of visiting family at the farm, despite the many changes. Mother and Dad enjoyed having all the family over for the holidays. In the summer, the siblings would have picnics at each other's houses. Grandchildren were being born and there were lots of birthdays and baptisms. It seemed wonderful to have the entire family so close. Everyone got along together and we had some great times. We were a close-knit family during those years.

One day Mother and Dad were contacted by the local school board. They wanted to buy ten aces of the farm on 23 Mile Road in order to build a new school. The plan would locate it right next to the property that Joe and I owned. We were asked if we would mind having a new school next door. I was thrilled to think that our children could attend school so close to home, so Dad and Mother sold the land for the construction of the new school building (Chesterfield Elementary School).

This initiated a new series of changes. Mother wanted to move to a larger farm, and Roland and Bertha wanted to go with them. Roland was having a hard time finding his niche in the work force. There were financial difficulties and Mom hoped the new farm might solve a number of problems for everyone. Dad and Mother could get some much-needed help to work the larger farm. They were moving once again back to Richmond.

# Chapter VIII

When I first saw the farm on Church Road, I was very happy for Mother and Dad. The house was huge. It looked like a castle! It had a big front porch with climbing rose bushes. The house was made of fancy concrete blocks and looked like a dream house. It had an inside bathroom and a beautiful kitchen. There were plenty of kitchen cabinets with glass cupboard doors. The house also had a big bay window for Mother's plants. The house featured sliding pocket doors that disappeared into the walls.

The barns were in very good condition. The milk house had all the equipment to ship milk to the creamery. They bought more cows to increase the milk base, as there were two families to support now. They were to share the work and the money with Roland and Bertha. The plan was to be real dairy farmers. They bought all new milking machines. The milk house had hot and cold running water with a new refrigeration system to keep the milk cool. They bought a very nice tractor and new farm equipment (plows, etc.) to operate the farm. The acreage went all the way back to the next road (Bethuy Road). The back of the farm was heavily wooded.

With every move, Mother and Dad hoped to make progress toward obtaining a better "roof over their heads." Each move required extra income. They struggled to make progress throughout their lives. It seemed that perhaps things might be easier for them now. When Joe and I first visited them, I was surprised to find out Mother and Dad were living upstairs (not on the main floor). Given the fact that Dad had his heart attack, it seemed unreasonable to expect him to climb the long stairway several times a day. Besides, the upstairs had no bathroom, kitchen, or running water. I expressed my concerns, but they were brushed aside. They were both very happy to have their two children living under one roof with them again. The plan was to build an upstairs bathroom and put in a sink with some cupboards for a kitchen. Mom felt everything was going to be just fine. I had hoped they wouldn't have to "rough it" in the new house. As they were nearing retirement age, it seemed only fair they live comfortably.

Meanwhile, Jerry was growing up and in high school. He and a few of his friends made some unfortunate choices. This devastated Mother and Dad. Considerable funds were needed for lawyers and court fees in order to deal with the circumstances. This was the first in a series of trying times for Jerry. Much to Mother and Dad's disappointment, Jerry also quit school. He was their last hope to see one of their children graduate. Jerry was also dating a girl named Janet while in high school. Their relationship became increasingly serious. Soon they wanted to marry. No amount of talking could persuade otherwise. Fearful that they would run away together, Mother took Jerry and his girlfriend to Kentucky to marry legally (in Kentucky you could get married at the age of sixteen). Jerry and Janet began their new life in Richmond living upstairs with Mother and Dad on the farm.

The farm in Richmond soon became a refuge for even more family members. Mary was now separated from her husband and was left with two small children and no place to go. Without income and support, Mother and Dad took them in. Catherine also stayed on the farm on occasions when she was ill and had no one to care for her children. The upstairs (which seemed so big in the beginning), was getting very crowded.

Life on the farm became contentious as many different personalities tried living together in limited space. Balancing work assignments became complicated as some members did more work than others. There were conflicts over drinking. There were other issues that were left unexplained but demonstrate how serious the family crisis seemed to be getting. Here's just one example.

Late one evening after I had put our children to bed, there was a knock on our door. Joe went to the door and discovered Mom, Dad, Mary and her children outside. Mother announced that they were going to need to spend the night at our house! It was apparent that Mom was very upset. Certainly they were welcome, but whatever had happened to cause this unexpected arrival? Mother indicated there had been an argument on the farm but refused to discuss the matter any further. Dad remained silent. Mary was having one of her panic attacks (which erupted often because of her marriage difficulties), and we attempted to call the doctor. A doctor was unavailable. Joe and I hurried to assemble some makeshift sleeping arrangements for everyone. We finally got Mary calmed down, and she went to sleep with her daughters in our family room. As I climbed into bed that night, I wondered why all this had taken place. It was so unlike Mom to come so late at night. This was one very strange and unusual event and spoke to the seriousness of the circumstance.

Bright and early the next morning they left as quickly as they came. There were few words spoken, and no one wanted breakfast. I never got an explanation as to what really happened. I knew the argument was too painful for Mom to ever speak of, and Dad was too faithful to share further details. I never brought the incident up again. I do know that several weeks later Roland and Bertha began building a house for themselves on a small piece of the farm's property. When their house was finished, Roland and Bertha moved out. Mother and Dad moved downstairs in the main house. At last, Dad and Mom didn't have to climb the stairs! Mary and the girls stayed upstairs. Jerry and Janet found a place to live on Fairchild Road.

Mother and Dad were still working at the hospital. They were putting in very long hours (between the hospital and the farm). In all reality it was too much for them. They needed a vacation! Dad and Mother tried to take some time off during the summer months. One summer they found out Aunt Anna and Uncle Tony were going to Ireland. Mother and Dad felt this was a good time to go too. Mom's other sisters had gone home to Ireland before, but Mother and Dad never had the time or the money. Now they were going to take the time. Mom was excited about going. She knew her beloved father and her mother would not be there, but the family farm could still be visited. Her younger brothers lived there now and were taking care of the farm. It now belonged to them. Mom would once again see the beautiful green hills of Ireland!

We were all very happy that they had the opportunity to go to Ireland. Mother got to see her homeland once again. The thought of Mom's homeland reunion gave me another idea. What if we gave Dad the opportunity to go back to his childhood home in Bangor, Maine? Joe and I asked them if they were interested in taking such a trip. Mother and Dad said they were, so Joe and I decided to make a family expedition of it (with our children as well). It had been more than thirty years since Dad and Mother went back east. Mom often talked about her early trip to Maine. She had described the high mountains and her fear of them. I was a little concerned about the mountains as well as I hadn't much experience traveling in high country either. Casting all concerns aside, the trip was scheduled for the following summer.

The trip back East was a memorable event for all. Dad wanted to stop along the way and see his two older children in Connecticut. He had seen his oldest son during the war, but wanted to see him again and meet his family. He had not seen his oldest daughters since he left as a young teenager. When we arrived at the homes of Dad's daughters in Connecticut, they gave us a warm welcome. Dad was near tears seeing his daughters after so much time had passed. It was a very personal and emotional time. Mother and Dad had written them over the years, but this was their first visit.

I felt strange meeting these sisters that I had heard about but had never seen. I was glad we went back east so that Dad could be reunited with his other children. It was worth the trip, and we hadn't even gotten to Maine yet!

The next morning we left for Portland, Maine. The objective was to meet Dad's son and his family. This became a rewarding experience for Dad and Mother as well. Over dinner everyone had the opportunity to become acquainted. The following morning we headed to the mountains in search of Dad's birthplace. The hills touched the sky, though the ride was not as steep as I imagined. We finally arrived. The clouds were so low it seemed you could almost touch them. If you looked in the distance there were actually some clouds below the high peaks. I know it frightened Mom years ago, but to me it was a majestic sight. It seemed so peaceful and quiet. Time seemed to stand still. You could hear the birds singing everywhere, and there were lots of big beautiful trees surrounding you.

Dad said that in his day you couldn't drive up the mountains in the winter. The only way to bring food to the cabins was with a horse and sled. His original family cabin was now gone, but Dad described it as being made of logs and having three rooms. There were no lights, just kerosene lamps. The water was drawn from a well outside and they used an outdoor toilet. Winters in Maine are very cold. One would not want to make too many trips outdoors in mid winter! I was glad that Mom seemed at ease throughout the trip. Returning to Maine now was much less stressful for her than it was thirty years ago with small children in tow. On the way down the mountain, Dad showed everyone the river that he and his dad used to float logs to the sawmill. The river had a strong current and you could almost imagine seeing the floating logs going swiftly by. He also showed us the place where he picked blueberries and where he played with boyhood friends. He was at peace recalling many of his childhood memories.

We drove through the small town of Bangor. Dad lived an important part of his life there with his Aunt Rose. He took us into the hardware store where he went as a boy. To me it looked like an antique store. Dad showed us where he worked as a projectionist, playing movies in the theatre. The building still stood in its original condition, though now very old. Dad said everything seemed the same as when he had left years ago. There were no new buildings of any kind. Time really had stood still in this quaint little town. We discovered where his Aunt Rose had lived before she died. Remembering that was an emotional experience for Dad. After all these years Dad remained convinced that his Aunt Rose was the only person in the world who ever loved him as a boy. The entire trip was a rewarding experience for everyone. We were happy to share in some of their early memories, as these memories are little treasures created from the history of their lives.

Soon after our travels were completed, it was back to work. Dad knew Mary needed a job in order to provide for her two young girls. He managed to get her hired at the hospital. Mary would work in the hospital lab as an apprentice. If she stayed long enough to gain skill and experience, she could someday become a lab technician. As Mary became established in the lab, she was able to get Catherine a job as well (first as an apprentice and later as a technician). In time Mary met and married a man named Stan. Mother and Dad liked Stan a lot. He was a businessman in Richmond and was successful. They felt he would care for Mary and the girls. Mary and Stan had a good marriage and eventually gave their two daughters a little brother. The family was happy for them all.

One day Dad went to work only to find out he was being replaced! The hospital was expanding, and the boiler equipment used in the facility was upgraded. Dad was never a certified boiler engineer. As the new equipment came online, the hospital looked for a more credentialed operator. Dad was devastated. He had been so proud and happy with his job. It gave him a feeling of importance in his life and that meant a great deal. While the hospital replaced him with a boiler engineer, they did say he could stay on and do odd jobs. The transition made Dad feel useless. Not knowing what else to do, he quit. He was nearing retirement age and felt this was the time to leave. It was sad that his job could not have ended with a real retirement. These were not the conditions he had anticipated. Dad became very sad and suggested that his ship would never come in. Mother quit the hospital soon after.

Working conditions on the farm did not seem to be improving. While the profits were being equally divided, there were challenges related to work assignments and shared farming responsibilities. Dad and Mother were putting in longer hours than they should have, especially given their age. They decided it was time to get out of the farming business. They kept their land but had an auction to sell off as much farming equipment and dairy cows as they could. Joe and I went to the auction to support them. Unfortunately, the outcome of the auction was not profitable. This was another disappointment and a sad time for both of them. Mom often remarked that they were at the end of a lifetime of hard work and seemed to have little to show for it. I felt their pain.

Dad's hay fever still bothered him a great deal every fall season. They now had a limited income (just Social Security and a little savings), and that made it difficult for them to travel up north. Mother and Dad decided to sell most of the property associated with the farm. They did keep some back property that bordered Bethuy Road. This land was divided into smaller lots. Mother and Dad kept one lot and gave each of their sons and daughters a lot as well.

Mother and Dad had no place to live and knew they needed to earn an income. The two of them took on a job managing a motel near Selfridge Air Force Base (now Selfridge Air National Guard). Their responsibilities included cleaning rooms and washing linens. Dad took on the night shift and would accept motel registrations. He preferred Mother not be left alone in the office at night. They lived in a small apartment off the office area. It featured a very small kitchen, bedroom, living room, and bathroom. They were allowed one day off per week. They worked day and night for the other six days. The motel had a shady reputation. It was known for its wild drinking parties and was quite the hot spot for secret romantic rendezvous. Mother and Dad didn't want to deal with all of that, so they didn't work there for very long.

They soon found another motel management job in the same area, but in a better location. Their responsibilities were similar to the first, as were their living conditions. I do remember the kitchen as being quite small but rather pretty. Joe was on the afternoon shift at the time, so we often had the chance to visit with them before our children came home from school. The four of us would sit together in the kitchen and have our tea time. I knew they were still uncomfortable with the number of secret affairs that the business attracted, but they stayed through the winter and into the spring. I felt badly for them and was sad to think they needed to do that type of work at their age in order to get by.

With money from the sale of the farmland, Mother and Dad decided to move up north permanently. They bought property in Cheboygan, on the Black River. It was high ground that overlooked the river. It was very scenic and quite beautiful. You could sit on the hill and watch boats going up and down the Black River. In order to get down to the river one had to walk down a rather steep hill. The river was wide, but on the other side was a large farm. It reminded Mother and Dad of their life on the farm. Dad constructed a small ranch home on this very beautiful piece of land.

It was sad to see my parents leave Richmond and head

north. I felt emptiness inside. I would miss them a great deal. When I discussed this with Mom, her response was, "Come and see us up north!" I knew we would, but it wouldn't be the same as having them close by and visiting them weekly.

It was especially hard for Dad to leave his children and grandchildren. He wanted to make sure there was a place for all to stay when anyone might come up for a visit. The ranch he built consisted of a large living room with lots of sofa beds and fold-up cots for guests to sleep on. There was an inside bathroom, a nice kitchen with hot and cold running water, and most of the comforts of home. I was happy they would have a nice home of their own. They were now living on Social Security (a limited income), and there was no money for "extras." They had just enough to get by.

Each summer our family would visit them during the July 4th holiday. Joe always scheduled his vacation for the big trip. We loved going up north, and the kids had great times. They had the chance to fish with their grandfather every day! Dad had built a fishing dock on the river. The fish the kids caught were never very big, but it didn't matter. Dad would clean them as the grandchildren watched by his side. Mother would take the fish and fry them up for dinner. Most of the time Joe needed to buy extra fish from a local fish market so that we had enough for everyone to eat!

There was always a July 4th parade in the town of

Cheboygan. Dad loved to go every year and looked forward to having us along for the holiday celebrations. Everyone enjoyed being together. I'm not sure who had the most fun, Dad or his grandchildren! He still loved to sing "little ditties" to his grandchildren and bounce them on his knees. This was getting harder though, and he would quip, "My legs aren't as strong as they used to be." These were very special times, and we were making precious memories to hold dear.

On one occasion we went into town to buy some groceries. The children were getting older, so we left them at home. It was a beautiful and carefree afternoon. We were just four adults going out for a ride, having a great time talking over old times. It was a very light-hearted moment with lots of laughter and joking. Mom (who never pried into anyone's personal business), asked me why I married Joe. This caught me off guard, and I was surprised by the seriousness of the question. I had to stop and think how to respond. Finally, I said that I was attracted to Joe because of his fun-loving personality. Mom smiled at me and I knew that Mother had seen in Joe what she had seen in Dad so many years ago. That was why she played the matchmaker when we were dating. I gained a new insight into Mom's wisdom.

On one of our trips up north, we wanted to take everyone to Mackinac Island. We had not been there before and were excited about going. We left early in the morning to spend the day. We crossed the "Big Mac" for the first time! I was not fond of bridges but made it over. Dad teased me all the way across in order to try and ease my stress level. The children loved the excitement and enjoyed the ride. We arrived in Mackinac City in order to make arrangements to take a boat across to the island. I was nervous crossing the bridge, but it was nothing compared to my nervousness in crossing open water in a boat. The boat we chartered was old and very slow (long before the fast, new hydroplanes of this age). Shortly after leaving the dock, the boat started taking on water (right near my feet). Dad called it to the attention of one of the boat workers. He indicated that the boat leaked all the time. That did not make me feel any better! Dad teased me and Joe joined in to help lighten up the situation. We finally got to the other side, but that boat couldn't get to the island quickly enough for me.

We spent a wonderful day on the island. There were so many beautiful things to see and shops to browse in. Throughout the day I said little prayers asking God to send us back on a different boat (that didn't leak). My prayers were answered! On other occasions we took trips at night to Fort Mackinac. We would spend part of the evening there waiting for darkness to fall. Then the bridge lights would come on. It was a beautiful sight and we enjoyed our trips to that area. Memories such as these are priceless. Spending time with family is a wonderful gift given by a loving Father.

Each year our vacation week went by quickly and we

hated leaving. If only these times could last a lifetime. When it was time for us to go, Dad would become emotional. It was hard for him to say goodbye. I took after my dad and had an equally hard time saying goodbye. Mom was always able to keep her emotions in check. Perhaps she left many of her emotions on the banks of the River Shannon, as she left Ireland many years ago. Dad would often call her the "strong one" in the family.

Mother and I exchanged letters weekly. There were also occasional phone calls. Mom spoke often about the severe winters up north. Winter took its toll on Mother and Dad. Often the snow was so high they couldn't get out of their driveway. Mom felt that if they needed medical help it would be nearly impossible to get it. They yearned for an end to long winters and warmer weather. They decided it was time to leave Cheboygan.

Dad and Mother moved back to Richmond and decided to occupy the one lot they had saved for themselves on Bethuy Road. They purchased an old house that needed to be moved from its original location. They hired a house-moving crew and relocated it to their empty lot. Dad often told Mom that one good thing came from their time away from Richmond. They were pleased that Roland was making progress and had taken charge of his life. He was handling his family responsibilities and was working a steady job. Dad was satisfied. He saw in Roland a better husband and a devoted father to his children.

In the early 1960s, we planned another trip east with Mother and Dad. This time we would visit Dad's other daughter, Dorothy. She and her family resided in Massachusetts. Dad had not seen her since she was a little girl, although they kept in touch through letters. The reunion was a very emotional experience for both. Dorothy was so happy to see her father again. She barely remembered him before she and her brother were adopted, but loved him from the start. Dorothy and Mother also got along well. Our families enjoyed spending time together. It was a rewarding experience for everyone. Now that Dorothy had met her father, she wanted to meet the rest of the family too. Everyone promised to keep in touch. Dorothy and her husband Clint were true to their word and eventually made several trips to Michigan in order to become acquainted with everyone.

As Joe and I watched our own family grow, a long-awaited dream of mine began to stir. I really wanted to go back to school in order to obtain my high school diploma. I know that Jerry also wanted to return to school. Jerry started attending some classes but began having difficulties in his marriage. Fortunately, I was able to register in an adult education program and make consistent progress. I would finally obtain the long-awaited high school diploma.

Jerry and Janet's marital problems seemed without solution. It was a very difficult time for Jerry, and over time it was apparent that their problems were irreconcilable. Divorce was imminent.

Jerry and Janet's divorce was a difficult blow to all involved, including Mother and Dad. They were especially concerned for Jerry and his boys and hoped Jerry might be able to retain custody of the children. As the family struggled to help Jerry redefine his life, it was clear that there were strong but varied feelings about what Jerry should do about child custody. Mother and Dad wanted Jerry to keep the boys and agreed to help him do so. This created considerable conflict between the other siblings and emotionally intense times followed. The family became divided in a variety of ways.

Jerry and I have always been very close. We shared the "youngest child" bond, and I tried to support Jerry whenever he experienced difficulties in life. Some family members were engaged in very serious discussions over issues that were really relevant only to Jerry. I felt that I was caught in the middle of a storm, especially when one particular meeting took place. Some of the siblings gathered at my house along with Mother and Dad. The discussions became very heated and argumentative. The debate would prove fruitless. It was always my intention to be supportive of Jerry's circumstances and also honor the feelings that Mother and Dad had. I think it is sad that support can be interpreted as "taking sides," and that the nature of our discussions ever had to take on such an adversarial mood. After the gathering ended, some implied I would "regret" the position I had taken.

The following week I received a phone call from a family member. This person told me I was no longer considered their sibling. I was in essence, "disowned." Argument and division can cause hearts to be hurt, and words used as weapons can be damaging. I know the wounds that I experienced were painful. I know the suffering that Mother and Dad experienced was even more devastating. It was a dark time in our family history, and the damage caused as sibling relationships weakened marked a turbulent trend not easily calmed. It would continue through the years.

Mom always maintained that blood is thicker than water, so Jerry and the boys moved in with Mother and Dad in the midst of difficult times. Joe and I continued our Sunday visits at their house. It is funny how things can change so quickly. Unlike the good old days when our entire family gathered with Mom and Dad, the family was now divided and refused to fellowship together. Some siblings took care to socialize at different times than we did. Mother and Dad hoped the feuding would stop and the storm would blow over, but it didn't. Conditions did not improve, and the wedge of division continued to fester.

Andy had moved up north and was removed from the scene. Catherine and Mary remained close. They were like-minded and enjoyed their work together at the hospital. Roland tried to walk a tight rope and be a bridge over troubled waters. There continued to be family parties between certain members of the family, but we were no longer asked to attend. Being a sibling no longer warranted an automatic invitation, unless the party was at Roland's house. The bonds within and among the original six siblings would remain strained for decades. Because I knew how hurt Dad and Mother were over family matters, I tried not to bring up sensitive subjects very often.

While it is true that Jerry's personal life was in turmoil, Jerry was not the cause of the sibling divisions that resulted. Quite the contrary! Jerry would successfully mend all relationships as the years passed. Mom was convinced that the root cause of all discord was the green-eyed monster that had been simmering beneath the surface for years. Now the dragon had really reared its ugly head and flames shot forth. It started fires that were soon out of control. As the years passed, the dragon would use any excuse to keep those fires from being contained or extinguished.

It was helpful to have goals, dreams, and plans in my own life. They helped me journey through these difficult years. Having gained my high school diploma, I started thinking about the idea of continuing my education at the college level.

Mother and Dad still longed for a special place to live in a warm climate. They soon bought property "sight unseen" in Florida. They had a pickup truck. Dad decided to build a camper on the truck bed. When that was finished they headed south to see the property they purchased in Florida. They decided they would live out of their camper. This would give them time to decide what to do after they arrived. Would Florida finally be the place of their dreams?

# Chapter IX

Mother and Dad loved Florida. Dad told the family they had found paradise. Their property was located in the country where it was peaceful and quiet. The subdivision had been recently established, but there were neighbors near them. Mother and Dad felt lucky to have found such a place. They decided to spend all of their winters in Florida.

They purchased a mobile home and placed it on their lot. Mother and Dad knew they would miss the family terribly and encouraged everyone to come down and visit. Dad had plans to build an addition on the mobile home so there would be extra room for everyone. The news made me feel very lonely. I would miss them a great deal. Instead of a few hours away from Richmond, they would be two days away by car. I would miss the bond between us, and it seemed things would never be the same. Despite my own sense of sadness I was happy for the two of them, especially Dad. Even though his ship never came in, I knew this would bring him much joy. Mother and Dad decided to keep their home in Richmond for the summer, and winter in Florida. The plan was to keep that schedule as long as they could afford both homes. Money was tight, and it was uncertain how long they could support two residences.

Upon returning to Richmond that spring, Mother and Dad decided to sell the house in Michigan. They needed money to buy building materials for the mobile home addition. They planned on building another house on the Richmond lot they had given to Jerry. Mother and Dad's house sold very quickly. We went to see them on a Sunday, and I was surprised to find out they had to be out by Monday! The new house on Jerry's lot was recently started. Just the foundation and floor were finished. On Monday morning I went back to see if I could be of any help. It was summer, so I brought the children with me. As we arrived, Mother and Dad had started putting up the walls. My young teenage son and I pitched in. My son had never done any extensive carpentry work and neither had I, but Dad did all the measuring and sawing. My younger daughter helped Dad by holding the wood as he cut it. One section at a time we were able to construct an outside wall. This was quite a feat for those of us unaccustomed to that kind of work.

I intended to leave around noon, as it was a very hot day. I suggested we all quit for the day, and Mom and Dad could come home with us. They could get in a nice shower, rest before dinner, and spend the night at our house. Mother would not hear of it. They intended on working till evening and would spend the night in their unfinished shelter! I was not happy about that. I reminded them they had no roof and only some of the walls were in place. Mom told me none of that mattered. I knew I couldn't leave them like that. We pressed on and spent the rest of the day working. We managed to box in the lower area of the structure with plywood in order for them to have some privacy that night and to keep the ground critters from wandering in. Fortunately it wasn't going to rain that night.

Before we left late that afternoon I tried once more to get them to come home with us. They would have no part of that, but Dad confided as we walked to the car that he never expected to get so much done in one day. I knew in my heart that Dad would have gone home with us in a second but would never go against Mother's wishes. Dad often referred to Mom as the boss (and sometimes one of the stubborn Irish).

That night I couldn't help but wonder how Mother and Dad were doing. It seemed they could never make an easier life for themselves. Dad was in his seventies, Mom in her sixties! I couldn't help agreeing with Dad. Mother just seemed to be too stubborn! I understood that they would never want to be a burden, or to put us out. Nonetheless, it seemed unreasonable not to come over and spend the night while building the new house. As I crawled into bed that night, every bone in my body ached. I was exhausted. I wondered if my son and daughter had as many aches and pains as I did. It was an uneasy sleep that night. I prayed Mom and Dad would be all right.

As Mom and Dad were committed to Florida for the winters, Joe and I decided we would plan our family vacations during Easter break. The children would be out of school, and I would not have difficulty scheduling my college classes around the holiday. The time frame would work well for all. On our first visit south, I could see why they loved it there. Dad and Mother had made a lot of friends and had quite a social life. There was a homeowners' club in the subdivision. Dad was elected president. There were many social events, and Dad and Mother went to them all. I was happy for their newfound lifestyle, as they actually got a chance to enjoy themselves! Most of their lives had been devoid of social activity and centered on work from morning till night.

Their mobile home had all the modern conveniences. It even had air conditioning. At last Mother and Dad could have an easier life, even though money was scarce. On one occasion I noticed Mom was taking special care in setting the dinner table for Easter dinner. She put out her nicest tablecloth, candles, and the best dishes she had. I felt Mother was going through a lot of extra work for just us. When I told Mom it wasn't at all necessary, Mother replied, "There's no sense in saving them for state days, bonfire nights, and Parliament Sundays." I asked her to repeat what she had just said. I thought I knew all of Mom's clichés, but this was a phrase that I had never heard before! I thought about this through dinner. I realized there were few occasions when Mother could have used the expression. For the first time in their lives they did have a few nice things for their Parliament Sunday!

I was also happy to learn that Mom was allowing herself a small luxury. She started getting her hair done. Before this she would never spend money on herself. She always went without for the sake of others in the family. Now it was getting difficult for her to do her own hair. I was pleased that Mother was finally spending a little money on herself.

During our Florida vacations we went on several day trips to all the classic tourist attractions. We had many wonderful times together, and our Easter vacations went by quickly. Whenever it was time for us to leave, it was very difficult for Dad. He still found it very hard to say goodbye. His eyes would fill with tears, and he couldn't talk. Mother was the strong one, hardly showing emotion. She had mastered the knack of hiding her feelings many years ago. I was like my dad and usually cried those first few miles on the return trip. I hated leaving my parents. I wondered how many years it would be before Mother and Dad would live in Florida year round. There would be even fewer opportunities to see them.

In 1971 our oldest daughter would be married. Mother

and Dad came down in early spring for the wedding. They were really looking forward to this special event. Polly (Dad's oldest daughter), flew in from Connecticut. She stayed with us. The night before the wedding there were the usual events (dress rehearsal, etc.) with lots of excitement. Polly and I had just finished clearing the table when the phone rang. It seemed that some of my siblings wanted to rehash issues that had caused so much family division in the past. I was told to show up for a sibling meeting or else! I was in a bad spot, and it seemed this was happening at a really bad time.

I talked this over with my family, and I determined that I had no desire to end up in a shouting match debating issues of the past. It just wasn't the proper time or place. Some of my siblings were infuriated and never showed up at my daughter's wedding the next day. Mother and Dad were very hurt and disappointed that some in the family would not let go of things long since passed. I could never quite understand the lengths to which some family members went to in order to avoid reunion. Mom would often indicate she felt that much of the division was rooted in jealousy. Fortunately we did have a wonderful time at the wedding, and the visit with Polly went very well.

For years Mother had a goiter. While we were vacationing in Florida one year it was decided that she should have surgery to remove the goiter. It had become quite large and was keeping her from getting a good night's sleep. There was breathing discomfort and difficulty swallowing. Because Mother knew we would be together over Easter, she chose that time to have the surgery. The day before she was to have the surgery, we went on an all-day trip to keep her mind off the upcoming operation. The last stop of the day included a visit to a shrine devoted to our Blessed Mother. It was very serene and beautiful at the shrine. Just before leaving, Mom and I went into the small chapel and prayed. After a few minutes I felt Mother wanted some time alone. I waited outside with the family. Mom remained inside for quite some time, but seemed at peace as we left. I knew the visit to the shrine gave Mother extra courage to face the next day.

Everyone went with Mother to the hospital the next morning. Dad could not bring himself to go inside, so my daughter and I accompanied her. When the surgery was over, I sent my daughter out to tell the rest of the family. Alone with Mom, I asked her how she was doing. She admitted to being in pain but asked me not to tell Dad that. Actually, I was surprised she had admitted her pain to me. That suggested that her pain must have been rather intense. When Dad walked in the room Mother was all smiles. "No problems," was Mom's standard answer when asked how she was doing. Today she maintained that tradition. I knew she was having a hard time fighting back the pain. Her body was tense as she tried to put on a good front. The doctor's orders only allowed us a brief stay, and as we walked away I could see the nurse giving

Mother a shot for her pain. I was happy to know she would be resting and sleeping comfortably now. We took Dad to see Mother every day. Each evening Dad would tell us how much it meant to them for us to be there. He said he didn't want to be alone without Mom. He was lost without her. Mother was able to come home the day before we left for Michigan. We were happy to be there for them during such a stressful time of life.

In time Jerry met and married a young woman named Marty. They would eventually have a beautiful baby girl. During the summer months, the house in Richmond got rather crowded, but Mother and Dad were happy and very fond of the new baby.

I had started my college career, which made Mother and Dad very proud. When we would visit them in Florida they would tell all of their friends that I was going to get a degree in education and become a teacher. I knew it was a dream for them to have a child graduate high school. To have a daughter in college really excited them, though I was somewhat embarrassed by all the nice things their friends would say to me.

Mother and Dad returned to Michigan one summer, and I asked if they would like to take another trip up north. Dad loved going on vacation with us because we would eat out in restaurants and Joe would buy dinner. Mom felt Joe was too generous with his money. After all our years of traveling together, Mother still lovingly scolded Joe for spending too much of his money on them.

On our very first vacation together, Mom felt we should have packed lunches. Joe would have no part of that! Of course Joe won that battle, and we always dined out on vacations. This was the only time Mother gave Joe a hard time, as she was very fond of Joe. We planned an extended trip north to several locations. The first stop was Tahquamenon Falls. We spent the day walking around the area and looking at the falls. It was very beautiful. We rented a large log cabin in the park with two bedrooms and a big living room with sofa beds. The teenagers slept on those. The cabin had a beautiful log fireplace, and the outside lot was surrounded by pine trees. Everywhere you went you could smell the scent of pine. It was the perfect location to stay overnight. That evening we walked to an ice cream stand and browsed through some shops. Mom rested at the cabin while we enjoyed a beautiful evening outdoors in the midst of nature.

The following morning we left for Copper Harbor on the tip of the Upper Peninsula off Lake Superior. The drive was absolutely beautiful. The highway had many twists and turns. You couldn't drive very fast. Both sides of the highway were lined for miles with trees that were beginning to change color. On arrival we visited Fort Wilkins (near Copper Harbor). The fort is right out on Lake Superior. We watched the big waves with whitecaps. The water on Superior was very rough. It was windy and quite cool. We enjoyed a long day in that area before heading back. It was a wonderful day together, but it seemed Dad enjoyed it the most. We stopped at several scenic places on our way back to the Lower Peninsula. The trip had gone on for a few days now. Our last stop before crossing the bridge was at another state park inside a national forest. It had a beautiful waterfall at the bottom of a very steep hill. It was easy walking down, but difficult coming back up! At the time I thought nothing of it. The weather was beautiful and it seemed one of those perfect days. The sun was shining through the trees, and there was a cool breeze in the air. There were birds singing everywhere. The park wasn't especially busy, and it was quiet and peaceful.

On the way back up the hill, the teenagers ran on ahead. You could hear their laughter echoing through the forest. What a happy sound. Dad loved to hear the young people enjoying themselves. Joe and Mom were walking a distance ahead. I stayed back with Dad. He was having a hard time walking the steep incline and was having a bit of difficulty catching his breath. We made frequent stops along the way as we were in no particular hurry. I did have some concerns about Dad as he was now seventy-nine years old. Nevertheless, he looked and acted much younger than his years. Still, I could not help but wonder how many more moments we would have with him. Might this be our last travel together? I was grateful for the wonderful time we were having as we made new memories together.

In 1974, Mother and Dad retuned to Michigan for

the summer, as was their custom. However, this would be a very special year. They would be celebrating their fiftieth wedding anniversary on September 20th. A big anniversary party was in the planning stage and there was great excitement. Joe and I thought it would be wonderful to take Dad and Mother on the honeymoon trip they never had. We planned a trip to Niagara Falls. Dad and Mother had often talked about going there if they would have had the money. Mother and Dad agreed to go with us. When our children heard of the trip, they wanted to go along as well. Our married daughter and husband (and their new baby daughter), our youngest daughter with her fiancé, and our son all decided to make the trip. Everyone felt the more the merrier!

Most of us were seasoned travelers by now and everyone knew what was expected as we traveled. We got along well together. This trip would be larger in number with new personalities added to the mix. It would be interesting to discover how well this would all work out. We decided to take two cars so that everyone could travel more comfortably. Our new son-in-law and our youngest daughter's fiancé had never really traveled to any great extent. As we crossed the border into Canada, we encountered heavy traffic, which complicated things. We struggled to keep the two cars together. There were no cell phones back then to help coordinate our location. There were concerns of being separated from the lead car, especially as not everyone was familiar with the route.

After a few hours on the road we stopped for lunch. The restaurants were so busy we were unable to find a place where we could all sit down and eat together. As we ate, we soon found out the reason why so many people were traveling. It was a Canadian national holiday! We knew we were in for more challenges as the day drew to a close and we needed to find lodging for the night. We made several stops only to find out there were no available places to stay. Our only option was to continue driving toward our destination. By late evening some were feeling quite anxious about the possibility of having to spend the night on the road.

Finally we discovered a large two-bedroom rental cabin. It was the last cabin available, so we decided to stay there. Our oldest daughter, husband, and baby took one bedroom. The single guys slept in the kitchen on portable cots. It was quite an adventure as everyone tried their best to get along amidst the stress of holiday travel. It was late by the time we finally got to eat a simple dinner.

The next morning we left for Niagara Falls. After a good night's sleep we were all able to laugh about our traveling escapades. The falls were beautiful! At night they were all lit up in different colors. We took many walks in and around the falls and had found a cute motel to stay in. It featured a large swimming pool and was located near shops and eateries. Everyone pulled together and we ended up having a great time.

Mother and Dad told us they would always have very special memories of our Niagara vacation.

Mother and Dad's fiftieth anniversary would be a special occasion for each of their children. The entire family had talked to Mother and Dad about the color of Mother's dress and Dad's tuxedo. Mom and Dad chose green as their theme, which left the daughters to shop for dresses in coordinating colors. The sons would have tuxedos like Dad's. Mother had her hair styled at the beauty shop and looked beautiful. She wore the beautiful jewelry that Dad had gotten her many years ago. I remembered the comment my friend had made back in school: "Your mother is beautiful!" I was proud to say she was right. Mom was a beautiful woman both inside and out.

Dad and Mother chose the menu for the event. I remembered how hard Mom worked the day of my wedding. I was happy that on this special occasion Mom could enjoy the festivities without having to work! Mother picked out her favorite song for the band to sing ("Danny Boy"). The band also played a Frank Sinatra tune called "My Way," which was a song dedicated for Dad. It was wonderful seeing them on the dance floor together as the band played these two special musical dedications.

There were lots of pictures taken that night. It was great having Polly come from Connecticut for the event. Dorothy and Clint made the trip from Ohio. Everyone had a wonderful time. I thought it was especially nice that all their family and friends from over the years came to celebrate the event with them. I am sure everyone went home with fond memories of the evening.

Fiftieth Wedding Anniversary
Katherine and Bill—September, 1974

Fiftieth Wedding Anniversary
Back Row Left to Right: Roland, Andy, Jerry
Front Row Left to Right:Rose, Catherine, Katherine, Bill, Mary
September, 1974

From the gifts they received, Mother and Dad wanted to give each of their children one of their presents as a gesture of thanks. They really appreciated the celebration we'd given them. Mom said they had received six different gifts. Each gift was twenty-four karat gold plated. I received a beautiful candy dish. It remains one of my prized possessions to this day. I wondered, though, how there came to be exactly six gifts. Did Mother and Dad help to make it that way?

I was sad as fall arrived and time drew near for Mom and Dad to return to Florida for the winter. I was already looking forward to spring when we would see them both in Florida. I was so thankful for the wonderful events that had taken place during their visit. I was especially thankful that God had kept them both in good health during the celebratory events. I was also grateful that the family divisions that so encompassed the family had been momentarily put on hold for the celebrations. Even Catherine and Mary seemed pleasant. Mother and Dad were thankful for that.

The Easter of 1975 found us traveling south to Florida with our entire family along for the ride. Our son-in-law was happy to know we would be staying with Mother and Dad and seemed relaxed. Mother and Dad were thrilled so many family members were coming down to see them. They had extra rooms and bedding because Dad had added on to the mobile home shortly after arriving in Florida. They would certainly have the opportunity to use that space now. We scheduled several day trips during the vacation, and one was to Busch Gardens. We wanted Dad and Mother to come with us, but they chose not to go this time. There would be a great deal of walking required throughout the park, and they felt it was too much. They encouraged us to go and have a good time. Off we went, but I had a heavy heart. This was the first time Mom and Dad did not accompany us on our day excursions. I knew they wanted to go but recognized at their age it would be difficult.

When we arrived at the park it started to rain very

hard. We had not yet paid our entry fee and wondered if we should go inside or not. Everything was outdoors except for the brewery. We waited for a while and were about ready to call it quits. Joe encouraged us to wait a little while longer. Anheuser Busch offered free beer at the gardens and Joe wanted to have his refreshment. Soon the rain stopped and the sun came out. It became very hot. Joe got his free beer, and the guys got a tour of the brewery. We enjoyed the beautiful gardens and spent a great day together.

Easter vacation went by quickly. Spring turned into summer, and I had a busy agenda planned. I had completed my undergraduate work at the university, but my bachelor's degree was not as marketable as I hoped. Jobs were scarce and there were few secondary teaching jobs available in Michigan at the time. I decided I might be more marketable with an elementary teaching certification. I decided to get a graduate degree and combine my master's with an elementary teaching certificate.

Dad and Mother returned to Michigan for the summer. I told them about my plan and the summer classes I would be taking. I explained the realities of the job market. They were happy I was not giving up on my professional goals and pleased that I was determined to teach. They did feel badly that I had worked so hard to get a degree only to find out that schools were not hiring teachers with my major. It was a busy summer! I was taking a class from the university and working with elementary children in an elementary school. The school I worked in had a large open classroom divided into sections. Each teacher had a section to teach. Some sections were empty as the enrollment was not filled.

One Friday I was walking back from the teacher's workroom. I had just duplicated some worksheets and assignments when a very unusual thing happened. I felt a very strong, powerful, force come over me. The power of it made me begin to fall backwards. I felt totally helpless. I fell toward the floor and ended up in a small chair made for little children. Amidst this overpowering force I got a very direct and explicit message. The message was, "Someone you love very much is going to die." I was incredibly startled by the event. The entire episode was very brief and took place in seconds. Despite its brevity, it was incredibly strong and factual. I had been walking through an empty section of the classroom where there were no children. I looked around to see if anyone had seen what just happened. No one noticed. Everyone was in the midst of their normal routine, and nothing seemed different.

I knew the force was a supernatural spiritual force. The message scared me. I thought back to when Joe left for service. I recalled the feeling that came over me about his not returning home. Was this message about Joe? I immediately began talking to God. It was awkward to pray as I was in the middle of my work and needed to return to the children. The remainder of the day passed in an ethereal way. The experience seemed to put me in a bit of a daze. What was I to make of all this? As the day ended and evening fell, the power of it all seemed to dim. I began to wonder if any of it really happened. As a precaution, I continued to pray for Joe's protection. I wanted no harm to come to him.

The weekend came and went. I was beginning to feel more relaxed as nothing bad seemed to be happening to anyone that I knew. Maybe it was just an oddity? Perhaps it really never happened? Very early Wednesday morning I got a call from Roland. He told me that Dad had died. I realized then that my message was about Dad and not about Joe. Dad died on June 18, 1975. My beloved father was gone.

Joe and I left immediately for Richmond in order to be with Mother. Mom shared with us about Dad's death. He never suffered and passed very quickly. He had been sitting in a chair waiting for Mom to get him a drink. He was not feeling well. When she turned around, he was gone. I asked what chair Dad was sitting in when he passed away. I walked over and sat in the same chair. A strange sense of peace came over me. I knew this was God's will. I knew God wanted to prepare me for my beloved father's death. I was comforted knowing this was His message. What a wonderful father Dad was. One could not ask for a better one. We shared so many special times together. It would be difficult to grieve his loss. I never told Mom about my experience with God and His message. When I recall the event even now, it puts me in awe.

*Rose Marie Rivard*

# Chapter X

Mother chose to stay with our family after Dad's funeral. We were happy to have her with us. Mom took the family room in the back of our house for herself. She would have her privacy and be able to rest or sleep whenever she wanted. Mother enjoyed being an early riser. She usually started her day with a cup of tea. I knew she wouldn't want to disturb anyone. Her thoughts were always about other people and never about herself. We went our own way during the day, and Mom had the run of the house. She was able to come and go as she pleased. Mother would help me prepare dinner in the evenings. She liked to peel potatoes. Potatoes were one of Mom's primary foods. After dinner we would wash the dishes by hand, even though we had a dishwasher. Mother loved to wash, and I would dry. This is what we did together through my teen years. I knew Mom was comfortable doing the dishes this way. Mother was very quiet during her stay and she cried very little. She did lose a great deal of weight, however. I knew it was grief that caused her to lose the weight. After a few weeks Mom went back to Richmond.

Mother stayed through the summer and decided Roland should drive her back to Florida for the winter. This would be the plan for the next several years. The family had some concerns about Mother's living on her own in Florida, but she would not hear of any other way. Mom was determined to keep her independence. I was very proud of the way that she was able to pick up the pieces of her life again and move on. I knew it was her great faith in God that gave her the courage to do that.

When Mother returned in the spring, I was just finishing my master's degree. I told her about a job I had accepted. I would be reopening a small Catholic school that had been closed for several years. Mom was very happy for me. We talked about the task of reopening the school in detail. Then I took her to see the school and gave her the grand tour. After we came home, Mom became a little sad and said, "Dad would have loved being here to see this." I put my arm around her and said, "He knows Mom, he knows." I knew in my heart that he really did know.

Now that Dad was gone, Mother's income became even more limited. I decided to give her a little money each month to help out with her bills. Roland and Mary also helped her out. Mother used the money Roland and I gave her for whatever monthly needs arose. Mary paid for Mother's telephone bill. The phone bill would soon become an issue of conflict, as Mary opposed the idea of Mom calling me. Mother became quite upset with Mary. If Mary was going to tell her who she could and couldn't talk to, then Mary could keep her money! I felt badly that Mom was put in that position, and I knew that even Mother's kind heart struggled with demonstrations of such obstinacy.

My son was older now and didn't always make the Easter vacation trips anymore. One year he did decide to go, and Mother asked that he drive Dad's brown van back to Richmond on the return trip. Our son was very happy to do this for his grandmother. They sat side by side in the big old van and got along great together. She wanted the van in Richmond so she could practice driving again. Dad had done all the driving in later years and there had been no need for Mother to do so. Now Mom had a renewed interest in driving so she could continue to exercise her independence. She was very determined to practice her driving skills, and no one was going to talk her out of it. It didn't matter that she was now seventy-seven years old!

Around this time we discovered Mother was having difficulty with her eyesight. I took her to see an eye specialist. We found out she had cataracts in both eyes and needed surgery. We took Mom to the hospital and the doctor took care of her, one eye at a time. There were several weeks between procedures. Mother stayed with our family while recovering. When she was feeling better and her eyesight was restored, I remember her saying, "I can see all the colors of the flowers on your table so much clearer now! I had no idea they were so beautiful!" I knew this was Mom's way of saying that the surgeries were worth the effort. I was happy for her.

In the area of Florida where Mother was living, the closest Catholic Church was in Silver Springs. It was called Our Lady of the Springs. This is where Mother and Dad went to church when they first arrived in Florida. It was a long fifteen-mile drive each way. After Dad passed on, Mother discovered the community wanted to build a church out in the forest near her subdivision. Mom was excited about this news and started to raise funds for the new church construction project. She would send me letters describing how she went from business to business collecting items to be auctioned off at parish events for fundraising. She was so happy to be involved in doing this work. She would tell me that on some days her van was so full of donated materials that she could hardly get any more in it.

Time passed and they began construction on the new church. It was called St. Joseph of the Forest Mission. The pastor was an Irish priest from the area in Ireland where Mother was born. Mom dearly loved him as he reminded her of her heritage. Mother was happy that she and her friends no longer had to drive so far to get to church. When Joe and I went down one Easter we were able to see the new church. Mother was so proud to have us go to St. Joseph's because she was so much a part of its beginning. Her fundraising efforts had been a substantial undertaking, especially for someone her age!

As I immersed myself in my work at the school, it seemed the yearly trips to Florida became increasingly difficult for me. I had been going to Florida for a number of years now, staying right up to the last day before going back to work. It seemed like the drive there and back kept getting longer and longer. My work in education could be exhausting. As the time for our yearly trip approached, I didn't look forward to the extended travel involved. Mother always said, "The grass always looks greener on the other side of the fence." I realized how true this was. I wanted a professional career for a long time. I worked for years at the university for my degrees. I searched long and hard for the right position. I finally had the career but also had all the tedium, effort, and never-ending responsibilities that went along with it. Professional jobs aren't always greener, just more stressful.

That Easter my oldest daughter and granddaughter decided to make the trip with us. We had only just arrived when Mom told me that she was having a meeting the night before we would be leaving. Mother was president of the ladies altar society, which consisted of about twenty women. She would have all of her friends there. Surely she wouldn't miss us if we left early? We could help Mother with her meeting plans. Then, we could make an early departure, and Mom wouldn't mind because she had a social function. In my mind that sounded like a plan that would give me a little extra rest before returning to my work-a-day world. I shared the plan with Mother, only to find her in tears at the thought of our early departure. I wasn't expecting that, so I immediately took back the suggestion and told her we would stay as long as we always did. I was exhausted and never fully realized how important this event was for Mom. She told me all about how she would conduct the meeting. She explained how she started her meetings with a prayer and we went over it in detail. It was a very beautiful prayer that she had chosen. She shared all the things on the meeting agenda. After lengthy discussion, Mom took her afternoon break.

I was devastated that I had made Mother cry. I went into the other part of the house and broke down in tears. I was so upset with myself. I told my daughter how terrible I felt. I had never made my mother cry before! I knew others may have done that in the past, but I never wanted to cause her an unhappy moment. I felt absolutely awful. To this day I wish I had never suggested we leave early. The thought was never intended to be hurtful, but still the words had made her feel sad. If only one could take back those moments in life.

Mother's meeting was very successful. My daughter and I played hostess while Mom introduced me to her friends. As I served the women their dessert, they spoke of how proud Mother was of me. They spoke of how delighted she was about my going back to school, getting my degree, and my work as principal of a Catholic school. Now I felt even more ashamed as I thanked them for their kind remarks. I realized Mom wanted me at that meeting so that they could meet the daughter she was so proud of. Mother also wanted me to be proud of what her accomplishments were. She was doing wonderfully. She was working for the church, became president of the ladies' church group, and had been an officer at the Lake and Forest club. How could you not be proud of her? She was someone to be admired.

During one of Mother's summer visits, she discovered a lump on her breast. A doctor's visit confirmed her concerns. He felt it was cancer and wanted to operate right away. Within days Mother was in the hospital awaiting surgery. All six of her children were there with her. After the surgery the doctors indicated the surgery was successful and that they had removed all cancerous tissue. Lab work would be needed to verify that.

Mother's sons went back to their jobs and planned to visit again in the evening. Catherine and Mary wanted to go out for breakfast. I invited myself along. I rarely ate a big breakfast but figured this was a special occasion. We went to a nearby restaurant. Seeing the family together brought back many memories. I thought of all the times Dad and I would go out for breakfast. I remembered his favorite breakfast (pancakes with blueberries), and I ordered a stack in honor of those memories. One wouldn't think that ordering breakfast could be confrontational, but the little things that could set my sisters ablaze often seemed odd. After the waitress left the table, Mary rebuked me for ordering pancakes. Mary was diabetic and felt I was offending her by eating pancakes with a sweet topping. I ate my pancakes, but they tasted bittersweet.

I decided to return to the hospital despite Mary and Catherine's objections. I knew Mother would be sleeping, but I wanted to be near her. I brought reading material and enjoyed the quiet time with my mom as she slept. These were peaceful moments of deep reflection. My thoughts went back in time, and I remembered so many years of struggle and sacrifice. The sacrifices and struggles that my parents endured were on behalf of family. They never gave up on the hopes and dreams they had for us all. Mom would awake from time to time and I was happy that I was there to give her immediate comfort and assurance. I remained at the hospital until Roland ended his work shift and returned to the hospital.

The lab tests confirmed the tissues removed were cancerous. The doctors believed they had removed everything problematic but still advised starting radiation treatments. These treatments would need to continue throughout the summer. This would be a trying time for Mother. All of this was hard for her to accept. She needed all the support she could get. Mother realized she would need someone to be with her. She asked one of us with emotional strength to volunteer for the duty. I knew it would be difficult for my brothers to take off that much time from their work. I knew Mary was also working full time. Catherine didn't drive. I never considered myself emotionally strong, but I knew I had the summer off. I told Mom I would take her. Mother had great faith in God. It would be faith that would get her through this ordeal. I joined my faith with hers in order for us to get through those days together.

The treatment center was in Troy. Traffic was very heavy (we hit rush hour every time), and it was a lengthy drive. Our first visit at the clinic was a long one, and I was concerned that it was taking so much time. There were strange "saw" noises coming from the room she was in, and I could not figure out what they would be sawing! When Mother was finally released for the day, I asked her about the strange noise. She managed a smile and told me they had to make a molded form. Then they had to fit it around the area where the radiation treatment would occur to protect some of the skin from getting radiation burns.

Other than that one conversation, we spoke little about her treatment. Mother preferred to make small talk about traffic and other chitchat. During these times I became increasingly aware of her tremendous inner strength and courage. I began to admire Mom in ever-increasing ways. It was a happy time when the treatments ended. She was physically exhausted, but her spirit was as strong as her faith in God. Mother (now near eighty), had made it through. She would remain on special cancer medicines for the rest of her life. The drugs were costly, and she had no prescription insurance. She paid $100.00 a month for the drugs while her Social Security income was only $475.00 a month. The financial circumstance was challenging.

Mother decided it was time to sell the house in Richmond. She would spend her summers in Michigan living with her sons and daughters. For the most part she stayed with Roland until he drove her south to Florida for the winter. The sale of the Michigan property helped Mother's financial condition. I accompanied her to the bank when she closed on the property. We spoke about her financial needs. On returning to Florida, Mother decided to open an account with the money from the house sale. This account would supplement her Social Security income and make it easier to pay her monthly bills.

Meanwhile, Jerry's second marriage ended in divorce. He became a single dad. He began work as an antique dealer and traveled extensively across the country. He also ended up spending a great deal of time in Florida. While in Florida, he stayed with Mother. Mom was thrilled to have Jerry and his daughter stay with her. The little girl bonded quickly with Mom, and she loved the little girl with all her heart. As a grandmother figure she was able to show Jerry's daughter much of the love and affection that she hesitated to show her own daughters, for fear of spoiling us (as she believed Dad did). It was a joy to see Mother with her granddaughter. They got along beautifully. They shared some very happy times together. Dad's death was an incredible loss, and I am sure these were some of the happiest times that she experienced since his passing.

One day, Mother's joy would turn to heartbreak. Jerry's daughter was taken away in a custody battle and returned to her mother. Mom later confided that the pain involved in this loss was so intense that she felt she was going to die. Mother missed her granddaughter incredibly. The separation was painful and she grieved the loss much like a death.

Mother had frequent visits by different members of the family while in Florida. Their families had grown, leaving the siblings with increased opportunity to get away from Michigan on vacation. Some of my brothers and sisters even purchased property in Mother's Lake and Forest subdivision.

Over the course of many long Michigan winters, I often felt that there would be opportunities to put family disagreements behind us. Whenever Christmastime approached, I reflected on the meaning of family and thought it would be nice to invite my sisters out for a holiday dinner. I knew the idea might be risky, so I suggested we go out for a meal (which would seem neutral ground for all). So many years had gone by. Was it naïve to think that there was still a chance for my sisters and me to become friends once again? Holiday seasons came and went with the same response to my invitations. Everyone was far too busy for dinner together. After several years of rejected requests, I finally stopped calling.

Mother would spend some of her summer with me. Andy came to visit her frequently during those times, and I was so happy to see him. My brothers were a valued link to family life. Unfortunately, Andy's health was failing. Mother would scold him because he continued to drink. Alcohol complicated his health issues, and he always laughed off her reprimands. He said he would never change. Andy was true to his word. As a result, he died at the age of fifty-five on April 6, 1984. Mother knew his life was cut short by alcohol. Had he taken care of himself he could have lived so much longer. My memories of Andy and Mother as the three of us visited together are special treasures. I would truly miss my brother.

Roland was now an important link in keeping ties with the family. He would call me from time to time in order to give me updates on family news. When there were family gatherings that I wasn't invited to, he would call me afterward and fill me in. Roland remained very close to Catherine. They shared the "oldest siblings" bond and were only a year apart in age. I know it bothered Roland to see conflict among sisters, but Roland was not one to rock the boat. He went along with whatever Catherine wanted. It was reassuring to know that I was always welcome at Roland's home, and when family get-togethers were at his house our family was always invited. I wasn't the most popular guest in town, but it was always nice to see everyone together.

Mother's sister had moved to Florida some time back. She felt blessed to have them living as neighbors. Aunt Margaret and Uncle Eddy shared much in their conversations with Mother, including discussions about last will and estate planning. They had already made out their will, and Mother was moved to get her affairs in order as well. Aunt Margaret and Uncle Eddie had made the oldest son and youngest daughter executives of their will. Mother determined that was a wise plan and did the same. Roland was the eldest son, and I was the youngest daughter.

Mother had the legal papers drawn up, though she never told me about whom she had identified as her executors. Mother came back to Michigan that summer and told the family that she had her last will legally filed. She identified Roland and me as executors and explained her reasoning. My brothers understood and it was not an issue of concern. You can imagine the impact Mother's decision had on my sisters! They became furious, and our strained relationships were stretched even more. Despite their objections, Mom had her mind made up, and there was no changing it.

The years continued to slip by. Mother was not getting any younger, and I felt it important to once again make the attempt to put family conflicts aside and make peace. I knew that would mean a great deal to Mom as well. After Roland brought Mother back to Michigan, she decided to stay at my house for a while. While she was staying with me I decided to invite the siblings over for lunch. Wouldn't it be great to surprise Mom with a family get-together! Roland had just made the long drive back from Florida and really wasn't up for socializing. Jerry was out of town. The remaining guest list consisted of my sisters and their husbands. I had set the date for a Sunday afternoon around 2:00 p.m. I prepared an extensive lunch, and the weather promised to be perfect. The time came and went and no one showed up. At around 4:00 p.m. one of my sisters pulled in the driveway. She told me they were not staying but wanted to see Mother in order to give her some clothing. I asked if she had forgotten about the luncheon.

As she walked out the door she sharply replied, "You didn't think anyone would really come, did you?"

In my heart I suspected they might not come for me, but I assumed they would make the effort for Mother. She was very sharp for her years. While I never told Mom about the luncheon plan, I think she knew what was going on. Between the prepared food, goodies, and the odd 4:00 p.m. "visit," I am sure she put two plus two together.

During one of our Florida vacations, Mother became quite ill. A doctor decided to hospitalize her. When Joe and I went to visit her in the hospital, we noticed she was hallucinatory. It was obvious that Mother was on a large variety of drugs. I was upset to see her so overmedicated. I had to walk outside the room to regain composure. As I roamed the hospital corridor, I noticed many of the patients were in a drug-like stupor much like Mother. I made inquiries with the nursing staff about Mother's condition, prognosis, and release. The nurse claimed she had no information and that I would need to speak with the doctor. When I inquired about the nature of the medical tests that they were conducting, I was also given very vague answers. I was becoming suspicious of the entire affair. There seemed too many "unknowns," and the medications set up red flags in my mind. I was very direct with the nurse and informed her that I expected to speak with the doctor the next day. I wanted a comprehensive medical report.

Joe and I arrived at the hospital the next day and found Mom waiting in the hallway. She was being released. She was completely off all medications and was happy and well. What would *you* make of all of this? Was Mother the victim of a senior health care scam, or was this an instantaneous healing? I do know the medical staff was really happy to see us go. I have since been wary of the ethical considerations given to seniors in some healthcare facilities.

Joe and I needed to return to Michigan as our Easter vacation was nearly over. Mary and Stan would now stay with Mother until she got her strength back. Mary and Stan arrived just before our departure. Stan was jovial but Mary was especially distant, choosing to avoid being in the same room with me. I could feel the resentment in the air.

The next year, Mother would be approaching her ninetieth birthday. Catherine, Mary, and Aunt Margaret decided to give her a special birthday party. It was held at the clubhouse that Dad and Mother had helped establish many years ago. What a fitting place for her birthday party! Jerry, Dot, Clint, Mary, Stan, Catherine, and Clarence all made special trips to Florida for the celebration. I was disheartened that we were not invited to participate. When we did return to Florida over Easter, Mother showed me photographs of the event. She was pleased that so many neighbors and family members came. I was very happy that Mom was honored on her ninetieth birthday.

About a year after this happy occasion, Roland told the family that he had been diagnosed with cancer. Mother was very concerned. She loved him very much and didn't want to see him suffer. She had been down that road herself and knew some of what he would have to go through. Mother accepted this as another one of life's burdens to carry for the Lord. She knew everyone had their own crosses to carry. She felt that how one endures trial is important. Mom was resolute in her faith and love for God.

Mother was always a very private person about financial affairs. This was true throughout her married life with Dad as well as through the years without him. She managed her own checkbook and paid her own way. You can see that I was naturally concerned when she asked me to review her checking account one day. She shared that it had been getting harder for her to keep up with the account and that one of my siblings had been assisting her. I could appreciate that, as Mother was now in her nineties. Mom's concerns were more worrisome, however. It seemed that a large sum of money had been withdrawn from her account. She indicated that one of the siblings "needed" it, but wasn't sure if she would be paid back or not. I decided to make some inquiries on Mother's behalf. We needed to clarify what the nature of the withdrawal was. Would these monies be replaced? My questions were not well received. I was accused of trying to control Mother's account and was told that her finances were none of my affair until after her death (as an executor). Somewhat concerned about these types of financial irregularities, I determined not to deposit money that I would give to Mom in that account.

It was clear that age was impacting a variety of Mother's abilities. When she would stay with Joe and me at our home, she struggled to climb the steps to her bedroom each night. On one evening she stumbled at the top of the stairs and hit her head on a door. She cut open her forehead and we needed to get her to the emergency room for stitches.

Dot and Clint came up from Ohio and a family gathering was planned at Roland's house. Roland asked me to drive Mother over to his house on Sunday. That would be awkward, as I was to drop Mom off, but not stay for the party. Roland was in a difficult position, and so was I. I mentioned to Roland that Mother might be a bit embarrassed about her stitches (they had to shave some of her hair), but that I would encourage her to attend. When Mother found out there was a gathering but that I was not invited, she was determined not to attend either. I convinced her to go without me and she finally agreed. She did stipulate that it would only be for a few hours. Joe and I dropped Mother of at Roland's. He greeted us at the door with great embarrassment. He looked at me helplessly and motioned to the family inside, saying, "Rose, I don't know what to…" I told Roland not to worry about it.

After the party was over we picked Mother up and asked her if she had a good time. Mom was quiet and rather ashamed of her children's actions. I felt very bad for Mother. It seemed she was always getting put in the middle of these awkward divisions.

There came a point in time when it seemed unrealistic for Mother to live alone in Florida anymore. She only made the trip when Roland had time to stay with her in the south. Beyond that, she would now spend most of her time in Michigan. During this transitional period I often had Mother over for dinner. Afterward, we had our tea time as usual. As Mom would begin sharing all her old stories about life in Ireland, I felt the urge to write some of those memories down on paper. I realized over time she might forget them. Later that night I went into my office and began writing the prelude to this book. Months passed, and I began to construct chapters one, two, and three. I used a tape recorder to help record some of the stories she shared, so that I could relate them accurately in my writings. It took effort to compile the materials, but my sense was urgent. It seemed time was slipping by.

My sister Mary died on June 8, 1993. Mother had now lost two of her children. She confided that she never expected to outlive them and was surprised to have lived as long as she had. Mom was doing quite well for her years, and I was very proud of her.

After returning from one of her last visits south with several family members, Mother informed me that she had given away her supplemental retirement account (the account set up to enhance Social Security income). I was quite surprised to hear that and asked her why she would do that. Mother replied, "Because they asked for it." I was not pleased to hear that. I knew that she now had nothing left except her monthly Social Security and the property in Florida. Mom had made it clear that the Florida property would be willed to Jerry after her death. What would Mother do if she needed money for some sort of emergency? Mom and Dad had worked hard all of their lives. They had always worked to have a roof over their heads, clothes on their backs, and food on the table. They were determined to be independent and never burden their children. They assumed they would have at least enough money to bury themselves. Mother didn't even have that anymore. There were no remaining cash assets. Mom was left with nothing! I found this all very depressing and called my youngest daughter in tears. She came over to the house and listened as I released the sorrow that I felt.

I was determined to do something about this situation. Because Roland was the other executor, I consulted with him. I suggested that an independent checking account be established for Mother so that her Social Security income could be directly deposited into that account and controlled with greater oversight. Roland realized this would not go over well with everyone in the family, but we proceeded with the plan. At least Mother would have enough income saved to pay for her own burial! I knew that it was important to her that she not be a burden to her own children. Her Social Security could also pay for medicine and daily necessities that she required.

I appreciated Mother in ever-increasing ways. She was extremely generous, giving away everything she had without concern for her own basic needs. It was not just money. She gave so much more than that. She was a living example of pure unselfishness. She gave of herself. She gave love to her family in unconditional and unquestioned ways. I was in awe of her capacity to love so completely. These were treasures few people ever acquire.

I was able to see Mother every week while she stayed with Roland. Time passed and Roland told me that Catherine wanted Mom to live with her for a while. That was a rare request, and not typical of the routine that had been established. I had some concerns about this arrangement. I was not welcome in my sister's home. How would I see my mom under these conditions? How long would Mother remain there?

With the move came a request that the allowance for Mother's living expenses be increased. I felt strongly that the expenses incurred at one sibling's house would be no greater than that at another sibling's house. There was no adjustment in the allowance, and I am aware that this was not well received by all. I was determined that Mother would have access to as much of the little income available to her. Beyond that, Mother was determined to pay for her own burial. That is one wish I wanted her to be able to fulfill.

Weeks would pass and Mother never returned to Roland's house. All were vague as to the length of her stay. It was out of the blue one day when my sister Catherine called me. She shared that she believed Mother was nearing death. She knew I would want to know that. I told Catherine that I wanted to visit with Mom right away but Catherine refused. She indicated she was having home-improvement projects done and that it was an awkward time for visitors. I found this irritating, as many of my other siblings had an open-door policy for dropping in on Mom. Catherine told me to stop by her house the next Saturday afternoon for a visit. I decided not to press the issue. I made Catherine promise that if Mom's medical conditioned changed or if death seemed imminent, I wanted to know right away. Catherine promised to keep me informed and agreed.

That Friday I was excited at the thought of being able to visit Mom the next day. It was May 26, 1995. I was settling in for the evening when the phone rang. Roland was calling with the news that Mother had just died. I was speechless. Why hadn't someone called before now? Joe and I were only minutes away from my sister's house. We left immediately. Catherine was standing outside in the yard when we arrived. I went inside to be alone with Mother for a few minutes. I was in such despair at not having had the opportunity to see my mom one last time and say goodbye before her passing.

Roland arrived shortly after we did. I was in tears as we gathered in the living room. I asked Catherine why she didn't call me. Catherine responded that she thought Roland would have done that, because he had been there the last two nights when it seemed Mom wouldn't make it to the next morning. I looked to Roland, who had a helpless look on his face. He could only say, "I didn't know...I didn't know." I was distraught and frustrated that the promise to keep me informed was never honored. I couldn't bring myself to stay any longer. I walked out the door, brokenhearted. My beloved mother was gone.

Even today my heart is torn and my eyes tear when I recall these events. I often wonder if Mom wondered where I was in those final hours. Did she wonder why I didn't come to her? How long and how hard it must have been if she had been waiting for me. I long to have had the chance to see her one more time and tell her how much I loved her.

# Epilogue

We have journeyed through the lives of my mother and father. In many ways you have journeyed through my life as well. Mother's life is one of courage, strength, and dedication. Her priorities were God, family, friends, and community. Her life was one of constant giving. She asked little, if anything, in return. I consider my mother to be among the great heroines in history. While not famous or rich in material things, she was rich in so many other ways. She had impeccable values, high standards, and a passionate concern for the rights of others.

Many books have been written about well-known individuals who have contributed much to the world. I feel Mother and Dad are equally great. Their story represents the life of many common people who have struggled through life's many hardships. They could be anyone's parents. Their lives illustrate a commonality we can all relate to as we recognize how we are bonded in our human condition.

I give to you my mother and father. Their story has been written from the heart with my greatest love and respect. Make them a part of your own life. They will help you understand your purpose in life. They will encourage you to become your very best. They will teach you about a love that is never disappointing. They will look for the best in you and stir you to excellence. If you reach for fame and fortune and happen to find it, they will be very proud of you. If you struggle and your ship never comes in, they will respect you with equal measure. They offer you love regardless of the circumstances in your life.

Mom has been a great inspiration in my life and someone I truly love and admire. She was a rare jewel. She was a gift that I want to share with you. She was a treasure that is part of your heritage. When Mother entered her eternal home I know she took many gifts with her. Her arms must have been full. You may ask, "What gifts?" Certainly not material items, as God has no need of those. What did she take with her to heaven?

Her gifts to God were the burdens, hardships, and many crosses that she carried daily for Him. The smile she gave when she was tired. The silence she offered instead of complaint. The compassion she shared. The understanding she had for everyone. The love she never stopped giving. These are a few of the many things she offers God in heaven. She lived her faith in God. She practiced her faith through Mass and the Sacraments. She understood that the key to the door of heaven and its vast treasure is forgiveness! How can we be forgiven, if we ourselves can't forgive?

I believe that Mother can say to the Lord what St. Paul once said. *I have fought the good fight; I have finished the race; I have kept the faith* (II Timothy 4:7 NIV). The Lord will have answered her with this. *Well done, good and faithful servant! You have been faithful and trustworthy over a little; I will put you in charge of much. Enter into and share the joy (the delight, the blessedness), which your Master enjoys* (Matthew 25:21 AMP).

We are on our own journey. We need to gather gifts like these as well.

Each of us needs to set our goals with our eternal home in mind. Like Mother, we hope to enter in with the same refrain. We can only pray that we hear the Lord's welcoming response. May He say to each and every one of us, *"Well done, good and faithful servant…"*

*Postscript*

I started writing about Mother's life in 1991. I finished chapters one, two, and three using my computer. I handwrote chapters four and five on a notepad while working one summer. I had the intention of entering those chapters into the computer at a later time. My career kept me very busy, and my progress was delayed for some time. After Mom died, I felt overwhelmed. To write about her life now was far too emotional. I had planned to do it "someday" in the future.

My someday was elusive, and the years passed. From time to time I would think about finishing the project. One day I was using my computer, and it wasn't working like it should. I talked to my son about it, and he remarked that it was getting old. He fixed it as best he could but said it wouldn't last for long. I ignored the warning. A few months later I went to use the computer again and it wouldn't boot up. I tried everything to get it started but nothing worked. I was about to give up when all of a sudden I realized that the only copies of the chapters for Mother's book were on that hard drive!

I didn't think I could begin to recall all of Mother's life as a little girl. I panicked. What would I do? I talked with God and asked Him to start that computer up one more time. If it would start, I would stay right there and print every page so that I would have a hard copy. I also told God that I would try and finish the book. I never promised Him that, because I wasn't sure if I could really get it finished! So many years had gone by. I believe He knew I would need His guidance. I tried turning on the computer one last time. It worked! I finished printing all of my early work. In the spring of 2007, I began to write again, on a new computer. Today is August 29, 2007. I have finally finished this "race."

# listen|imagine|view|experience

## AUDIO BOOK DOWNLOAD INCLUDED WITH THIS BOOK!

In your hands you hold a complete digital entertainment package. Besides purchasing the paper version of this book, this book includes a free download of the audio version of this book. Simply use the code listed below when visiting our website. Once downloaded to your computer, you can listen to the book through your computer's speakers, burn it to an audio CD or save the file to your portable music device (such as Apple's popular iPod) and listen on the go!

How to get your free audio book digital download:

1. Visit www.tatepublishing.com and click on the e|LIVE logo on the home page.
2. Enter the following coupon code:
   c6f0-d512-5d77-78b8-d4e9-e3c6-2826-0c6f
3. Download the audio book from your e|LIVE digital locker and begin enjoying your new digital entertainment package today!